VICTORIANA
A Miscellany

Edited by
Sonia Solicari

Guildhall Art Gallery, London

First published in Great Britain, 2013
by Guildhall Art Gallery
Guildhall Yard
London
EC2V 5AE

Designed by Crescent Lodge
Printed in England
ISBN 978-1-9027-9515-7

Guildhall Art Gallery is part of the City of London Corporation.

CITY
OF
LONDON

www.cityoflondon.gov.uk

Frontispiece
Victoriana by Otto von Beach. © Von Beach

Edited by

SONIA SOLICARI

VICTORIANA
A Miscellany

being the

Accompanying Publication

to the

Exhibition at the Guildhall Art Gallery

Victoriana: The Art of Revival

7th September to 8th December 2013

The WHOLE COPIOUSLY ILLUSTRATED by
OTTO VON BEACH

and forming an

Indispensable Companion to neo-Victorianism
for Gentlemen & Ladies

The Book Designed by
Crescent Lodge

Textual editing by
Tim Killick

It has been the greatest of pleasures to work with all the contributors to this book. I would like to thank the authors for their diverse and nuanced interpretations of neo-Victorianism, and Otto Von Beach for his unwavering patience (well, he was frozen in Russian ice for 114 years!). His contribution has been generously supported by the Friends of Guildhall Art Gallery, Vivien Knight Fund.

I would also like to acknowledge those individuals who have eased the passage of this book, from conception to print, with their help, advice and astounding generosity. These include: Barnaby Barford, Tony Bennett at Knockabout Comics, Ligia Bouton, Ellie Charman at Stephen Friedman, John Coulthart, Alannah Currie, Tessa Farmer, Dan Hillier, Jane Hoodless, Piers Jamson, Stephen Kenny, Ayla Lepine, Tristan Lund at the Michael Hoppen Gallery, Lynda Nead, Kevin O'Neill, Tabitha Philpott-Kent at Marlborough Fine Art, Chantal Powell, Paula Rego, Carmon Reynolds, James Robertson, Rob Ryan, Patrick StPaul, Phil Sayers, Yinka Shonibare, Richard Slee, Bryan Talbot, Timorous Beasties, Mark Titchner, Yumiko Utsu, Tom Werber, Mathew Weir and the Alison Jacques Gallery, Carole Windham, and Libby Wright.

Last but not least, I express my gratitude to Lynda Brockbank at Crescent Lodge for entering into the spirit of the project with great knowledge and gusto, and to Tim Killick for whipping those en-dashes and semi-colons into shape. As ever, thanks are due to Jeremy Johnson who keeps things shipshape at Guildhall Art Gallery and London's Roman Amphitheatre whilst I embark on such projects as this.

The Editor

Acknowledgments	4	
Illustrations to the work	6–8	
A Welcome from the Editor *Sonia Solicari*	10–14	
Jane Eyre and Dorian Gray *Cora Kaplan*	16–30	*Iconical*
Conversazione *with Sarah Waters*	32–37	*Conversational*
The Victorians *Matthew Sweet*	38–41	*Personal*
Demonstrative Digits *Catherine Flood*	42–47	*Directional*
Neo-Victorian Things: A Scrapbook *Sonia Solicari*	48–62	*Ornamental*
The Lost Property *Lee Jackson*	64–68	*Fictional*
A Neo-Victorian Alphabet *Otto Von Beach*	70–77	*Observational*
Steampunk *Katty Pearce*	78–83	*Socio-cultural*
The Graphic Novel *Tim Killick*	84–92	*Visual-verbal*
Wireless Time Travel *Paul St George*	94–103	*Telegraphical*
Neo-Victorian Tattooing *Matt Lodder*	104–12	*Epigraphical*
Lace *Tom Gallant*	114–24	*Sensual*
Shades of Modern Gothic *Gilda Williams*	126–38	*Historical*
Notes on the contributors	140–42	

A Welcome from the Editor

Figure 1.1
Yumiko Utsu, *Octopus Portrait* (2009).
C-type print. Copyright the artist.
Image courtesy of Michael Hoppen
Contemporary and G/P Gallery.

Figure 1.2
Dan Hillier, *Mother* (2006).
Altered engraving. Copyright the artist.
Image courtesy of the artist.

Jane Eyre and Dorian Gray

From Paula Rego, 'The Guardians',
from *Jane Eyre*. Lithographs.
Copyright the artist. All images
courtesy of Marlborough Fine Art.

Figure 2.1a
'Jane Eyre' (2001–02).
Figure 2.1b
'Crumpled' (2001–02).
Figure 2.1c
'Up the Tree' (2002).
Figure 2.1d
'In the Comfort of the Bonnet'
(2001–02).
Figure 2.1e
'Loving Bewick' (2001).
Figure 2.1f
'Mr. Rochester' (2002).
Figure 2.1g
'Undressing' (2002).
Figure 2.1h
'Biting' (2002).
Figure 2.1i
'Come to Me' (2001–02).

Figure 2.2
Yinka Shonibare, *Dorian Gray* (2001).
11 black and white resin prints,
1 digital lambda print. MUSAC
Collection. Copyright the artist.
Image courtesy of Stephen Friedman
Gallery, London.

Demonstrative Digits

An album of demonstrative digits.
All photographed out and about by
Catherine Flood and Nicola Swann,
August 2012–April 2013, unless
otherwise stated:

Figure 3.1a
New North Press, *Reverting To Type*
(2010). Letterpress exhibition poster in
black and red. Copyright the artist.

Figure 3.1b
Ambient advertising sign on the
pavement outside Kings Cross Station,
London.

Figure 3.1c
Steward outside the Olympic Park
during London 2012 Games.

Figure 3.1d
Signpost on Kensington Road, London
made in 1911 and still in situ.

Figure 3.1e
Packaging for Dr Stuart's tea-bags.

Figure 3.1f
Sign on the wall of the clothing shop
White Stuff in Salisbury.

Figure 3.1g
Postcard by Crispin Finn at the 2013
Pick Me Up graphic art fair, Somerset
House, London. Copyright the artist.

Figure 3.1h
Stephen Kenny, *Disappear Here* (2010).
Letterpress print. Copyright the artist.

Neo-Victorian Things: A Scrapbook

All images courtesy of the artist, unless
otherwise stated.

Figure 4.1
Mark Titchner, *I Want a Better World,
I Want a Better Me* (2012). Digital print.
Copyright the artist.

Figure 4.2
Ligia Bouton, *The Adventures of William
Morris Man: William Morris vs. Owen
Jones 1* (2011). Coloured pencil, ink,
graphite, gold leaf, collage on digital
print. Copyright the artist.

Figure 4.3
Richard Slee, *Grill* (2010). Ceramic and
Metal. Copyright the artist. Image
courtesy of Hales Gallery. Photograph
by Zul Mukhida.

Figure 4.4
Piers Jamson, *The Drawing Room*
(2009). Photograph. Edition of 5.
Copyright the artist.

Figure 4.5
Timorous Beasties, *Devil Damask*
(2007). Flock Wallpaper.
Copyright Timorous Beasties.

Figure 4.6
Jake and Dinos Chapman, *One Day
You Will No Longer Be Loved XX*
(2008). Oil on canvas. Copyright the
artists. Image courtesy of White Cube.
Photograph by Stephen White.

Figure 4.7
Miss Pokeno, *Trophy Chair* (2009).
Chair with taxidermy.
Copyright the artist.

Figure 4.8
Tessa Farmer, *Swarm* (detail) (2004).
Mixed media. Copyright the artist.

Figure 4.9
Patrick StPaul, *Whisper in the Midst
of Silence* (2011). Mixed media.
Copyright the artist.

Figure 4.10
Chantal Powell, *Siren* (2010).
Bird cage, spray paint, artificial flowers.
Copyright the artist.

Figure 4.11
Jane Hoodless, *Pteridomania Contained*
(2012). Transfer-printed cloth,
greyboard, cast metal. Copyright the
artist.

Figure 4.12
Rob Ryan, *I Remember, Nobody
Remembers* (2010). Earthenware with
hand-painted and printed decoration.
Copyright the artist.

Figure 4.13
Carole Windham, *Dearly Beloved*
(2013). Earthenware with enamel
decoration. Copyright the artist.

Figure 4.14
Mathew Weir, *Hangman* (2010).
Oil on canvas, mounted on board.
Copyright the artist. Image courtesy
of the Alison Jacques Gallery.

Figure 4.15
Barnaby Barford, *Damaged Goods*
(2008). Film still. Copyright the artist.

Figure 4.16
Losers, *Flush feat. Riz MC & Envy*
(2010). Dir. Tom Werber; artwork Dan
Hillier. Film still. Image courtesy of
Dan Hillier and Tom Werber.
Copyright the artists.

Figure 4.17
Phil Sayers, *Shalott (after J. W.
Waterhouse)* (2008). Combination
of 5x4 transparency and digital
photographs. Copyright the artist.

Steampunk

Figure 5.1
John Coulthart, *Steampunk* (2008).
Text by Jeff VanderMeer.
Vector art. Copyright the artist.

Figure 5.2
Author G. D. Falksen shown with
mechanical arm created by Thomas
Willeford. Photograph by Tyrus Flynn.

The Graphic Novel

Figure 6.1
Alan Moore and Kevin O'Neill, *The
League of Extraordinary Gentlemen,
Volume I* (London: Titan, c.2000),
title-panel to Issue 1. Image courtesy
of Titan.

Figure 6.2
Bryan Talbot, *Grandville Bête Noire:
A Fantasy* (London: Jonathan Cape,
2012), p. 30. Image courtesy of
the artist.

Figure 6.3
Ford Madox Brown, *Work* (1852–65).
Oil on canvas. Manchester Art Gallery.

Figure 6.4
Alan Moore and Eddie Campbell,
From Hell (London: Knockabout
Comics, 2000), ch. 8, p. 40. Image
courtesy of Knockabout Comics.

Wireless Time Travel

All images courtesy of Paul St George.

Figure 7.1
*Development of Wireless Telegraphy.
Scene in Hyde Park, Punch Magazine*
(26 December 1906), p. 451.

Figure 7.2
George Du Maurier, *Edison's Telephonoscope (transmits light as well as sound), Punch's Almanack for 1879*, [unpaginated].

Figure 7.3
Paul St George, *Design for the Telectroscope* (2008). Illustration by Felix Bennett. Copyright the artist.

Figure 7.4
Paul St George, *Square of oppositions showing relationships between science, deception, the occult and insanity.*

Figure 7.5
Illustration of Geißler tubes and Crookes tubes, taken from Meiser & Mertig, *Preisverzeichnis No. 27, Physikalischer Apparate und chemischer Geräte* (catalogue of physical and chemical apparatus and devices) (Leipzig, 1903).

Neo-Victorian Tattooing

Figures 8.1a & 8.1b
Tattoo Flash Designs by Quyen Dinh (2013). Copyright the artist.

Figure 8.2
'A German lady, well known in society', in 'Pictures on the Skin', *English Illustrated* (April 1903), p. 105. Copyright the British Library Board.

Figures 8.3a–8.3d
Neo-Victorian Tattooing by Rebecca Marsh, aka Tiny Miss Becca (2013). Copyright the artist.

Lace

All images courtesy of Tom Gallant, unless otherwise stated.

Figure 9.1
Tom Gallant, with Marios Schwab, *Dress 09* (2008). Laser-cut corded silk, printed crêpe. Crafts Council Collection. Copyright the artists. Photograph by Alex Lee.

Figure 9.2
108 Moths (2004). Cut paper, glass. Copyright the artist.

Figure 9.3
Detail of *Iris* (2012). Digitally printed vinyl wallpaper. Copyright the artist. Photograph by Sophie Mutevelian.

Figure 9.4
Fuji Under Clouds (2010). Cut paper, glass. Copyright the artist.

Figure 9.5
Firecrest (2006). Cut paper, glass. Copyright the artist. Photograph by Andy Keats.

Figure 9.6
Chrysanthemum (2005). Cut paper, glass. Copyright the artist. Photograph by Andy Keats.

Figure 9.7
Chrysanthemum (2005). Cut paper, glass. Copyright the artist. Photograph by Andy Keats.

Figure 9.8
That Same is He (2011). Cut paper, wood, veneer, glass, paint, varnish. Copyright the artist. Photograph by Tessa Angus.

Figure 9.9
Would I to Those (2009). Cut paper, glass. Copyright the artist.

Shades of Modern Gothic

Figure 10.1
View of the Palace of Westminster, from the River Thames (c.1851). Lithograph. Copyright the City of London.

Figure 10.2
Lyonel Feininger, *Kathedrale* (Cathedral) (1919). Woodcut. Museum of Modern Art, New York. Gift of Abby Aldrich Rockefeller. Copyright the artist's estate. Image courtesy of the Museum of Modern Art, New York/ Scala, Florence.

Figure 10.3
Dorothea Tanning, *A Mrs. Radcliffe Called Today* (1944). Oil on canvas. Private collection. Copyright the estate of Dorothea Tanning, ADAGP, Paris and DACS, London.

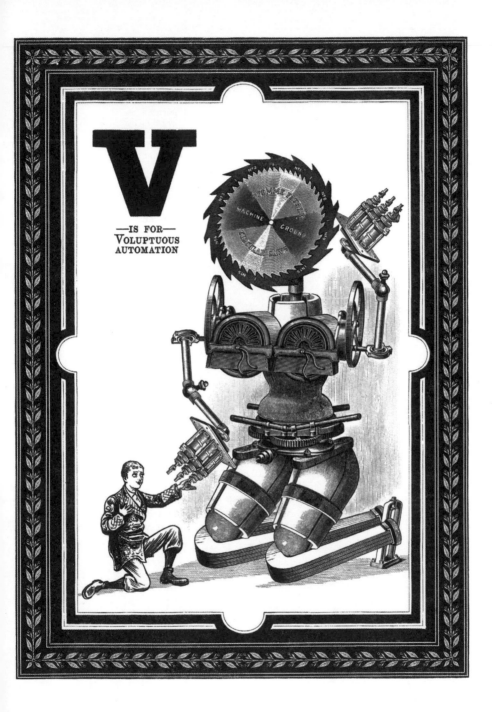

A WELCOME
FROM THE EDITOR

SONIA SOLICARI

Octomaids are woman–mollusc hybrids that have crawled and slithered their way into the contemporary artistic imagination. From Japanese manga to fashion photography, their popularity recalls the Victorian fascination with the mermaid (think Edward Poynter and J. W. Waterhouse) and raises similar questions about our negotiation of femininity and of social versus natural. I could think of no better way to begin my introduction than to dwell for a moment on these creative subversions. Part Jules Verne, part drawing room, the resulting cross-breed is hyper-modern and undoubtedly unnerving. The painted Victorian lady of Yumiko Utsu's *Octopus Portrait* has the face of a gleaming, oozing, white marine-mask and Dan Hillier's *Mother* appears only mildly flustered by her searching, reaching tentacles that offer a menacing alternative to the encaging skirts of the period (Figs 1.1 & 1.2). These images suggest the enduring appeal of the Victorians, who continue to embody the cliché of prim order barely concealing a dark underbelly of animalistic impulse.

(FIG. 1.1)
YUMIKO UTSU,
OCTOPUS PORTRAIT (2009).
C-TYPE PRINT.
COPYRIGHT THE ARTIST.
IMAGE COURTESY OF
MICHAEL HOPPEN
CONTEMPORARY
AND G/P GALLERY.

(FIG. 1.2)
DAN HILLIER,
MOTHER (2006).
ALTERED ENGRAVING.
COPYRIGHT THE ARTIST.
IMAGE COURTESY OF
THE ARTIST.

1.2

1.1

Welcome to *Victoriana: A Miscellany*, in which leading artists, writers, academics and curators have responded to the idea of the Victorian in contemporary culture and teased out its challenging dualities: familiar and threatening, retrograde and progressive, sentimental and confrontational. This assemblage of theory, observation, art and literature forms the companion, but by no means the catalogue, to the exhibition *Victoriana: The Art of Revival* at the Guildhall Art Gallery – 7 September to 8 December 2013 – which brings together the work of artists and designers of the last twenty years who have been inspired by the nineteenth century.

For the title of both the exhibition and this miscellany, we are in debt to Cora Kaplan, whose study *Victoriana* freed the word from its 'corner antique shop' connotations and created a platform from which to examine, across disciplines, the contemporary response to our Victorian past.[1] The work of Ann Heilmann and Mark Llewellyn has similarly drawn the boundaries of neo-Victorianism in their oft-quoted but indispensable definition: 'To be part of the neo-Victorianism we discuss […], texts (literary, filmic, audio/visual) must in some respect be self-consciously engaged with the act of (re)interpretation, (re)discovery and (re)vision concerning the Victorians'.[2]

This practice of self-conscious engagement with the past lies at the heart of Victoriana. It is about looking forward as well as back and about historical fluidity as well as stubborn interpretations of the Victorians that are more about us than them – what about those covered piano legs! Arriving at even this loose remit for both exhibition and publication has been a long journey on a road of inspirational resurgence that is littered with the corpses and haunted by the ghosts of revivals past. From the 1920s onwards, there have been several discernible revivals of Victorian style: from ironic Oxford students enthusiastically embracing the 1840s, to 1960s psychedelic reworkings of art nouveau. Current and recent revivals, by which I mean the last two decades, look at the Victorian period through this long lens – clouded by generations of reinterpretation.

This extended view is taken by Gilda Williams's 'Shades of Modern Gothic', which explores how modernism appropriated the Victorians, creating a visual culture of awe and wonder that is essentially architectural – a building up of references and inspirational sources that brings us to where we are today. From the macabre to the surreal, the lure of Victorian Gothic underpins recent revivalism, drawing on the imaginative legacy of iconic literary characters such as Jane Eyre and Dorian Gray. These pervasive subjects form the basis of Cora Kaplan's essay which examines, through the work of Paula Rego and Yinka Shonibare, those giants of subverted Victorianism which loom large in twentieth- and twenty-first-century feminism and gender theory.

I have taken the editorial liberty of including my own piece, 'Neo-Victorian Things: A Scrapbook', which casts an eye over material culture and the experience of living with the past made modern. From taxidermy to Staffordshire figures, the proliferation of neo-Victorian 'stuff' in contemporary art and culture raises questions around what the nineteenth century means to us. This query is responded to in Matthew Sweet's essay 'The Victorians', as his everyday footsteps trace the Victorian streets. Sweet's personal experience echoes Charles Dickens's urban rambles, but also suggests the environmental ties which bind us to the Victorian experience.

Catherine Flood's metropolitan enquiries have exposed her to the visual signposts that point the way around both the neo-Victorian city and the contemporary graphic environment. The demonstrative digit also suggests the return of the hand-crafted graphic, as witnessed by the recent letterpress revival, and probes the function and future of design in the digital age.

These layers of past, present and future are revealed and concealed in artist Tom Gallant's fascination with lace. Gallant uses contemporary design tools to tease out historic pattern and ornament, addressing ideas of both fashion and identity and their inherent evasion of meaning, alongside a darker exploration of oppression and vice. Matt Lodder's essay similarly explores the possibilities of adornment through the medium of tattooing and the indelible marks of an unconventional Victorian aesthetic.

Questions of who we are, where we come from and where we are going have inspired Katty Pearce's review of the Steampunk phenomenon – a neo-Victorian counter-culture that is in turn politically progressive and socially regressive. Steampunk not only offers an alternative platform for the negotiation of fashion and identity in a post-industrial world but filters our fascination with technology through a fantasy lens. This obsession with Victorian technologies also informs artist Paul St George's essay, which looks at the inventions the Victorians never realised. His work is driven by a desire to give the Victorians, posthumously, the creations they craved. This anachronistic vision of the past is at the heart of the graphic novel explosion, as presented in Tim Killick's contribution. From Alan Moore to Bryan Talbot, our view of the Victorians is now complicated by retro-future superheroes and a parallel world of anthropomorphic invention.

The relationship between fact and fiction, the original and the reimagined has infiltrated the popular contemporary consciousness through the neo-Victorian novel and its subsequent televisation, as seen in the work of writer Sarah Waters. In our *conversazione*, Waters reflects upon the recent literary plundering of the Victorian past and our appetite for nineteenth-century sensation. It is thus, with particular pleasure, that I present a neo-Victorian short story by writer and nineteenth-century obsessive, Lee Jackson. 'The Lost Property' tells the tale of a Victorian lady's neglect of her possessions against the backdrop of the burgeoning railways.

Last, but by no means least, I introduce the work of artist Otto Von Beach, whose extraordinary neo-Victorian biography is not to be overlooked on the contributor's page. Otto's double-take illustrations offer a graphic perspective on the past. With his usual attention to detail, he has produced for us a neo-Victorian alphabet covering all the pertinent points of the perceived movement.

It has been a pleasure to work with all of the contributors to this project and the image permission-granters who have helped to make it such a visual feast. I hope that the resulting miscellany proves a useful companion to Victoriana in all its complexity and reflects, above all, the spirit of playfulness and experimentation that accompanies even the more sensitive and challenging aspects of our desire to look back.

1 Cora Kaplan, *Victoriana: Histories, Fictions, Criticism* (Edinburgh: Edinburgh University Press, 2007), p. 3.

2 Ann Heilmann and Mark Llewellyn, *Neo-Victorianism: The Victorians in the Twenty-First Century, 1999–2009* (Basingstoke: Palgrave Macmillan, 2010), p. 4.

I

—IS FOR—
INDOLENTLY
INTREPID

JANE EYRE AND DORIAN GRAY

CORA KAPLAN

In the opening pages of Charlotte Brontë's *Jane Eyre* the child, Jane, is turning over the pages of *Bewick's Book of British Birds*. The pictures rather than the 'letterpress' draw her to Bewick, but his introductory description of the 'death white realms' of the 'Arctic Zone' give 'significance' to the images – 'the rock standing up alone in a sea of billow and spray [...] the broken boat stranded on a desolate coast [...] the cold and ghastly moon glancing through bars of cloud at a wreck just sinking' – albeit the 'shadowy' and 'half-comprehended' 'notions' of a 'child's brain'. For Jane, 'Each picture told a story; mysterious often to my undeveloped understanding and imperfect feelings, yet ever profoundly interesting'. In nineteenth-century literature the child's imagination, accorded poetic power by the Romantics, was given a certain license to run riot. The terrors and cruelty, no less than the playful inventions of a child's imaginary world, created a space for an alternative aesthetic and also other narratives borne of fantasy and rich with melodrama, more memorable, often, than Victorian fiction's conventional endings. Here, images and narratives became touchstones for infantile storytelling in which the Gothic, grotesque and the supernatural are given free rein, evading the moralising imperative of Victorian culture.

The aesthetic present in two brilliantly provocative revisionings of Victorian classics, Paula Rego's *Jane Eyre* (Figs 2.1a–2.1i) and Yinka Shonibare's *The Picture of Dorian Gray* (Fig. 2.2), turn text into image, resonating powerfully with Victorian versions of the child's imagination as a wide-ranging, uninhibited, synthesising force. The same 'childlike' pleasure in writing the self into told or read stories can be seen in Shonibare's 'replacement' of Oscar Wilde's ever-youthful protagonist with his own image in *Dorian Gray* (2001). 'All little girls improvise', Rego has said of her lifelong passion for making images from stories, 'and it's not just illustration: I make it my own'.[1] The opening scene of Brontë's novel is the inspiration for 'Loving Bewick', one of the most arresting and disturbing lithographs in Rego's *Jane Eyre* (2002), in which a pelican loosely held by the adult Jane has its large beak in her mouth (Fig. 2.1e). The pelican, needless to say, is not one of Bewick's British birds, and this departure, as well as the substitution of the grown woman for the novel's girl-child, is typical of the liberties that Rego will take with Brontë's work across the series, disrupting its already complicated chronology, subtly introducing her own history into its topos. For both the Portuguese–British Rego and the British–Nigerian

Shonibare, cosmopolitans to the core, these novels about the English and Englishness by writers of Irish descent are ripe for the reinterpretation of nationality as well.

Of the twenty-five images in *Jane Eyre*, some are more easily associated with passages in the text than others. Although stories – other people's and her own – are essential to her work, they act, much as Bewick's prints do for Jane, as catalysts for her active, wilful imagination. 'Loving Bewick' relates to two earlier prints by Rego which involve close and unsettling encounters between women and birds, a congruence which evokes the many Renaissance versions of a nude Leda and the Swan.[2] The pelican, a more homely, nurturant bird, who, in legend, would wound her own breast and use the blood to feed her young, coupled with the buttoned-up Jane with her mouth open, actively asking to be fed, certainly domesticates the image yet in a particularly unsettling way. This is a scene of mutuality, and as Marina Warner suggests, there is a note of 'true nurturance' in it, symbolic of the way in which 'mind food', the 'books and pictures' that Bewick represents, offer Jane a means of survival. However, a sense of something odd and uncomfortable in this surreal intra-species engagement remains, as it does in some of Tenniel's illustrations of Lewis Carroll's *Alice in Wonderland*. Unlike the nude Leda or the diminutive Alice, Jane is depicted as a fully dressed grown-up in what might otherwise seem to be a child's fantasy, or a fanciful children's story. Whose imagination is this? The happy domesticity of the scene makes Jane and the bird seem more, not less unnatural, and more perversely sexual, the hybridity of its sources and its indeterminate genre making it a truly uncanny image. And in *Dorian Gray*, Shonibare deploys a related stratagem, normalising the intrusion of the artist as Dorian within the *mise-en-scène*, but in so doing provoking the discomfiture of the viewer, testing the limits of what his audience can find culturally tolerable.

Playing about with the originals and their afterlives in this way is the signature of Victoriana in visual art, film and narrative. Those who cite famous nineteenth-century works typically depend on a palimpsest of text, image and critique that form their legacy. *Jane Eyre* and *The Picture of Dorian Gray* have become so well known that they have taken on the status of modern folktales. Transgressive in their own day, shocking still, if for different reasons, in ours, their plots are part of the cultural capital of anglophone readers. For Rego and Shonibare the Victorian texts become the starting point for multilayered works which include key references not only to adaptations and retellings, but also to art and story in earlier and later historical periods.

Paula Rego tells us that she came to *Jane Eyre* through Jean Rhys's dystopian prequel, *Wide Sargasso Sea* (1966), in which the Caribbean-born novelist creates a sympathetic backstory for Brontë's most disturbing creation, Bertha Mason, Rochester's mad, dissolute white Creole wife. The repressive nature of Victorian society, so vividly present in Brontë's masterpiece, recalls, for Rego, the Portuguese Catholic culture of her youth. These parallels govern many of the chosen themes of the twenty-five lithographs in the series – a merging of her own history and memory with her reading. The artist's depiction of Bertha in the *Jane Eyre* series as a dishevelled, sexualised but still recognisably female figure, owes as much to Rhys, and to a number of Rego's earlier prints and paintings of eroticised, disturbed women, as to Brontë, for whom the Bertha incarcerated in Thornfield is already a degraded 'thing' rather than a gendered human.

Shonibare's *Dorian Gray* is more selective in its appropriations. Drawn primarily from the 1945 Hollywood adaptation of Wilde's novel directed by Albert Lewin it owes very little, in any obvious way, to Wilde's original.[3] The photographs are, with one exception, restaged stills, tongue-in-cheek imitations that introduce a commentary on scenes from the film, placing the artist in the role of Dorian. Homoerotic attraction is a powerful subtext to the novel's plot – the prosecution in Wilde's trials used *The Picture of Dorian Gray* as evidence of his proclivities and practice. The film cuts all but one of these oblique references, and Shonibare's *Dorian* omits them entirely, the first a decision presumably based on contemporary censorship, the second, perhaps, because attitudes have changed so profoundly. Yet both film and artwork rely on the common knowledge of Wilde's sexuality and his downfall, for which his novel retroactively provides a cruel, moralising parallel: it is there in our cultural memory and expectations whether the neo-Victorian text chooses to display or conceal it. Shonibare's photographs shift the ground beyond parody and pastiche, by highlighting the circum-Atlantic movement of British and American texts, daringly replacing the idealised white 'western' beauty of Wilde and Lewin's ageless 'Dorian' with a black man. Though the work goes much deeper in its critique, the initial effect of this substitution is to call into question the premise on which both novel and film rely – that the lure of male

(FIG. 2.2 OVERLEAF) YINKA SHONIBARE, *DORIAN GRAY* (2001). 11 BLACK AND WHITE RESIN PRINTS, 1 DIGITAL LAMBDA PRINT. MUSAC COLLECTION. COPYRIGHT THE ARTIST. IMAGE COURTESY OF STEPHEN FRIEDMAN GALLERY, LONDON.

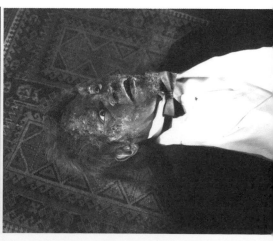

beauty as defined by a given culture blinds those who come in contact with it.

In a related way, Rego's resistance to the dominant Anglo-Saxon aesthetics of beauty echoes Brontë's detestation, expressed through the child Jane, of the culture's adoration of children with 'pink cheeks and golden curls' whose faults are easily excused. Yet the artist's radical depiction of the nineteen-year-old Jane makes her not only plain – 'little', 'pale', and with features both 'irregular and marked' in the words of the novel – but much older, stockier and with a face worn by suffering. It may be that Rego's Jane picks up on and emphasises the fact that the narrator is an older, wiser Jane who relates and interprets, 'from the distance of […] many years' the voice of the child, adolescent and young woman. Nevertheless Rego's unsentimental interpretation of Jane's physical attributes destabilises audience recognition, breaking our identification with Jane Eyre as we have previously known her, and highlighting our unconscious complicity with a still-reigning aesthetics of femininity.

Paula Rego was in her mid-sixties when she began the work on *Jane Eyre*, and the premature ageing of Jane might be understood as part of her sympathetic relationship to the heroine – but one that stops well short of self-portrait. The visual or referential presence of the artists in these two works is never straightforward. Neither Rego nor Shonibare seem overly interested in Charlotte Brontë or Oscar Wilde as historical figures, or even as writers whose 'autobiography' is an element of their most celebrated fictions. Narrative Victoriana often overuses the trick of eliding the nineteenth-century writer's biography with their novels, producing composite texts that are a variety of bio-fiction. Rego and Shonibare substitute the artist's presence for the writer's history, but the effect is very different, challenging rather than embracing the authenticity of the autobiographical. I would argue that Rego's use of place, objects and scenarios from her own peripatetic life in *Wide Sargasso Sea* and *Jane Eyre*, and Shonibare's pre-emption of the protagonist's role in *Dorian Gray* serve a more exemplary than a strictly personal function. The merging of Rego's twentieth-century Portugal with Jane's England is one way of expressing Rego's fascination with Brontë's heroine, but it also works to universalise the elements of Brontë's novel that interest the artist, and are the overarching themes of her oeuvre: dysfunctional and abusive families, the sadistic nature of relations between men and women, adults and children and, sometimes, women and women.

In Rego's world (as in those of Charlotte Brontë and Jean Rhys) the social and psychic are never comfortable places to be, and children and women are born to suffer. Without the 'costumes', which are nevertheless of great importance to her work, the story, Rego suggests, could take place elsewhere and in different periods. Some of the 'Victorian' trappings of the *Jane Eyre* series are superficial – only clothes deep – while others, especially those depicting the classroom and refectory at Lowood School are more fully embedded in the visual and literary iconography of nineteenth-century Britain, evoking Dickens's as well as Brontë's unsparing criticism of English educational institutions. In-your-face artifice problematises what we might think of as the historical or the autobiographical in these texts, for the seeming attention to historical detail is often mischievously misleading or manufactured – the nineteenth-century costumes that dress the women in *Jane Eyre* are taken from a cache of family clothes from Portugal, and props are hired or made in the artist's London studio. 'Mr. Rochester' (Fig. 2.1.f) is played by Rego's friend and frequent model in a rented outfit on a hired plastic horse accompanied by a stuffed dog. The print cheerfully emphasises the immobility of the animals. While Rochester's physiognomy faithfully reproduces Brontë's initial description of him – 'dark face', 'stern features', 'heavy brow' – an expression somewhat 'ireful' – the composition of the lithograph is deliberately theatrical, formulaic and still, reminiscent of tableau or illustration. But it is no less resonant as a result, since it works on the viewer less as a new version of the novel's surly, sexy love interest, than, unusually for the series, as an aide-memoire to past encounters, a reminder that we have already 'met' Mr Rochester in story, illustration and on screen.

All Rego's and Shonibare's images provoke us into thinking again about what we 'know' of these so familiar characters and their stories. Jane in particular is dramatically transformed. But of the figures in Rego's *Jane Eyre*, Rochester, named by Brontë after the seventeenth-century rake and poet, John Wilmot the 2nd Earl of Rochester, and evoking, for Brontë and Rego, the folk villain Bluebeard, is the least complex. Like the fake horse on which he sits in 'Mr. Rochester', Rego's anti-hero is at one level a hollowed-out figure, marking the social and psychic place of unyielding and potentially treacherous masculinity. The nine lithographs in 'The Guardians' on show at the Guildhall exhibition are a subset of the whole *Jane Eyre* series. 'Mr. Rochester' is the sixth print, appearing even later in Rego's work than he does in Brontë's novel. The figure he cuts in the series confirms what the images of Jane as child and woman have already indicated – that this is an anti-sentimental and anti-romantic take on Brontë's novel and its afterlife.

In Shonibare's *Dorian Gray*, masculinity, old and new, is a more problematic category altogether. Born in London in 1962, Yinka Shonibare grew up in Nigeria, returning to England to live and study at the age of seventeen. Paralysed only a year later with an inflammation of the spinal cord, he has lived and worked with disability for his whole career, conceiving art whose physical realisation is carried out by others. A self-described transcultural subject and a cosmopolitan citizen, his work explores, in a hugely inventive range of forms, the afterlife of colonialism, attacking the idea that 'people have to insist on one identity' – a belief that he calls a 'neo-nationalist [...] fantasy' associated with notions of 'purity'.[4] Eighteenth- and nineteenth-century iconic art and narrative have had a particular appeal for him: *Mr and Mrs Andrews Without their Heads*, from 1998, places the mannikins in the same position as they are in Gainsborough's famous portrait of 1750, dressed in the style of the period, but with their clothes crafted from the Dutch wax-printed cloth with Indonesian batik motifs that was marketed to colonial subjects in Africa and come to be associated with 'authentic' African design.

Robbed of the agency invested in their aristocratic looks and gaze, we focus on the costumes, which suggest the complex combinations of capital, technology, conquest and trade that were the sources of English wealth, power and cultural value, as well as the fictions of identity that support them. These virtual beheadings are the complement to *Dorian Gray* and a closely related photographic work, *Diary of a Victorian Dandy* (1998), where the head, the artist's own, forms the central conceit. *Diary* uses late-nineteenth-century dress, but its scenes are based on William Hogarth's early-eighteenth-century paintings *The Rake's Progress* (1733). Known by his attention to his clothes, the dandy, a creation of the late eighteenth century mimicked the aristocracy, gaining entry to society through his wit and style – a self-fashioned, entirely self-regarding figure, admired as well as ridiculed, but often seen as doomed, like its original, Beau Brummell, who squandered a fortune and died in a lunatic asylum. The dandy throughout his reign across the long nineteenth century is a more light-hearted, less personally culpable figure than the rake, and is sometimes seen as the origin of late modernity's celebrity.

Shonibare however takes care to tie them together. The dandy may be a prime example of cultural creation and the invention of tradition, a wonderfully mobile figure without obvious class or cultural markers, but Shonibare will not simply celebrate him, in either his early or late incarnations.

As in *Dorian Gray*, in *Diary of a Victorian Dandy* the role of the dandy/rake is taken by the artist, his head shorn of his signature dreadlocks. Both the *Diary* and *Dorian Gray* follow London life through the activities of self-constructed louche, corrupt and corrupting male figures, each on a downward spiral. In scenes of gambling and prostitution photographed in detailed period sets, *Diary* is an exuberant depiction of some of the scandalous activities that are only hinted at in Wilde's novel and Lewin's film. *Dorian Gray*, like Rego's *Jane Eyre*, depends on the audience's prior knowledge of fictional plots to be narratively legible. We see Dorian/Shonibare first, not in person, but in an early sketch of the fatal picture in the drawing room of the artist Basil Hallward, whose walls are hung with eighteenth-century aristocratic portraits. Next he is presented with his back to us looking at himself in a gilt-edged mirror. Both these images reference strategies of self-portraiture in fine art, Shonibare's presence in the scenes merging the figures of artist and dandy as engaged in a common project of self-creation and projection. Two groups of photographs drawn from the film establish Dorian as a man at ease in the pub/music hall where he meets the singer Sibyl Vane who he will seduce and abandon, as well as in the country hobnobbing with aristocratic friends. The central set of images show him first in the London fog encountering Basil Hallward, and later stabbing him to death. The final set of three photographs subtly revise both novel and film by skipping the crucial scene in which Dorian confronts and attempts to slash the vile portrait, and in so doing returns it to its initial record of his youthful beauty, his action destroying its subject instead, so that his lifelong transgressions are now written as they should be, on the body.

In Shonibare's reworking, the transformation of Dorian occurs without reference to the painting. Instead, in a scene of his own invention, we see Dorian looking once more in the gilt mirror, encountering his true image, grotesque, unkempt and aged, followed by two further photographs faithful to the film: the shocked discovery by friends, and his body on the floor. Like the excision of Basil's erotic fascination with Dorian, Shonibare's demotion of the

2.1A

2.1B

2.1C

2.1D

2.1E

2.1F

2.1G

2.1I

(FIG. 2.1A)
'JANE EYRE' (2001–02).

(FIG. 2.1B)
'CRUMPLED' (2001–02).

(FIG. 2.1C)
'UP THE TREE' (2002).

(FIG. 2.1D)
'IN THE COMFORT OF THE
BONNET' (2001–02).

(FIG. 2.1E)
'LOVING BEWICK' (2001).

(FIG. 2.1F)
'MR. ROCHESTER' (2002).

(FIG. 2.1G)
'UNDRESSING' (2002).

(FIG. 2.1H)
'BITING' (2002).

(FIG. 2.1I)
'COME TO ME' (2001–02).

portrait as the symbolic centre of the story – it is significantly left out of the title of the work – has the effect of leaving more room for the self-authorising role of the dandy as performance artist. The preoccupation with style and surface of a metrosexual culture and aesthetics, the work suggests, is no longer so rule governed that the binary between what is hidden and what is revealed, or the distinction between life and art, even the racial hierarchy that would necessarily exclude a man of African descent, no longer exists. *Diary of a Victorian Dandy* and *Dorian Gray* replay the history of modern masculinity through selected representations of men behaving badly in societies that simultaneously encourage and punish their excesses. Through its parodic appropriation of cinematic melodrama *Dorian Gray* may mock the easy moralism of both Wilde and Hollywood, but if anything it widens, rather than narrows, the ethical questions the story raises for us today.

Rego has said that she admires Jane because she is 'disciplined and determined', containing her 'passionate nature' and using 'good sense and intelligence' to survive, a judgement not so distant from Brontë's own.[5] In 'The Guardians' the first five prints are of Jane but are not in sync with the novel's chronology. We see Jane first as an adult, from the back, her face hidden, her gown black and enveloping making her look broad rather than slight. Only something in the lock escaping from her pinned up hair and the movement of her arms, as if presenting herself for approval suggests that she is vulnerable and young. In the second, 'Crumpled' (Fig. 2.1b) she is a child lying full length as if flung on a floor, recalling the scene early in the novel when she is locked in the Red Room by her aunt's servants. Even horizontal her body is rigid with rage, her hands clenched – a less than abject victim of adult persecution. In 'Up the Tree' (Fig. 2.1c) she is an adult in a child's posture, resting, eyes shut. The print exploits the amusing idea of a Victorian woman in voluminous skirts hoisting herself on to a branch in search of peace and refuge. The comic poignancy of the image is checked and undermined by the sinister cruciform shape of the dead tree and Jane's awkwardly dangling feet. The next print shares something of this poignancy but in a less overtly symbolic mode. 'In the Comfort of the Bonnet' (Fig. 2.1d) shows Jane at a pause in a journey, her weary, starkly featured head resting on her hand and in the impromptu security of the hollow of her hat. The Victorian costume occupies much of the dark space in these images – protecting, enclosing and disciplining the central figure at the same time. In contrast, prints seven and eight, 'Undressing' (Fig. 2.1g) and 'Biting' (Fig. 2.1h), show Bertha, first disrobing watched over by her keeper, the servant Grace Poole, and in a white dress which does nothing to hinder her brother's assault. Rego's assistant and model Lila sits for both Jane and Bertha. Their features are very distinct, but their difference throughout the series is more materially marked by the minimal nature of Bertha's clothing, leaving her exposed but unappealing. Bertha's attitudes in particular, but some of Jane's as well, recall the pictures of the hysterics in Charcot's asylum in Salpêtrière.

In Rego's art, even more than in Brontë's or Rhys's fiction, it is hard and dangerous work being a woman; in *Jane Eyre* performing femininity is visibly exhausting, leaving little room between repression and madness for adult females to negotiate a sense of freedom and agency. In Brontë's proto-feminist novel the reward for restraint and discipline coupled with ethical resistance was a happy heterosexual reunion. If, in life and fantasy, Victorian regimes of gender were harsh, they seem even harsher in Rego's more dystopian imaginary. The final extraordinary print in 'The Guardians', as well as the last chronological reference to the novel in Rego's *Jane Eyre* shows an agonistic Jane against a blaze of fire, answering Rochester's supernatural summons 'Come to Me' (Fig. 2.1i). For those viewers who know the book, the fire economically represents the burning down of Thornfield and the death of Bertha. Speaking of the image, Rego makes her intention clear: 'she goes to him. But she'd better have her doubts of course. It's not such a good deal. But she does go to him, and that's supposed to be a happy ending. It is. But here I put her doubting.'[6] Rochester and Jane will have to struggle on as they can, but there is no doubt about the happy outcome of the marriage between Brontë and Rego. Yet Rego's salutary scepticism about human happiness, her fierce critique of both the past and present that resists any self-congratulatory idea that with modernity comes progress, is bracing rather than defeating.

Rego's and Shonibare's work is evidence that the move from story to visual art succeeds in remaining playful and innovative while keeping a critical and political edge where too often narrative Victoriana disappoints. A utopian energy runs through and underpins *Jane Eyre* and *Dorian Gray*, both remarkable re-articulations of the creative tensions in Victorian fiction's ostensible realism, its Gothic elements and its larger mythopoetic ambitions.

1 Cited in Marina Warner's 'Introduction' to Paula Rego, *Jane Eyre* (London: Enitharmon Editions, 2004), p. 9.

2 See *Girl Swallowing Bird* and *Woman and Maribou* in T. G. Rosenthal, *Paula Rego: The Complete Graphic Work* (London: Thames and Hudson, 2013), p. 295. The image is also related, as Rosenthal and Warner both suggest, to an etching and aquatint from 1989, *Baa, Baa, Black Sheep* (Rosenthal, p. 30), which depicts a large sheep in a modest but erotic embrace with a girl child.

3 *The Picture of Dorian Gray*, Dir. Albert Lewin. Metro-Goldwyn-Mayer, 1945. Produced by Pandro S. Berman, and starring George Sanders, Hurd Hatfield, Donna Reed and Angela Lansbury.

4 Yinka Shonibare interview, *Crossing Borders*, National Gallery of Victoria. Online: http://www.ngv.vic.gov.au/ crossingborders/interview/yinka_ interview.html. Accessed 1 June 2013.

5 Paula Rego, cited in Rosenthal, *Complete Graphic Work*, p. 166.

6 Ibid., p. 176.

C

—IS FOR—
CONCATENATION

CONVERSAZIONE, WITH SARAH WATERS

CONDUCTED VIA THE MEDIUM OF
EMAIL ON 15 FEBRUARY 2013

Your first three novels were set in Victorian London – is there something about the nineteenth-century city that particularly taps into our hopes and fears?

It seems to me that the Victorian city lends itself to storytelling in a very exciting way. It's a city that's modern enough to feel close to us, to have lots of overlaps with our own experiences of urban life, but its landscape is full of more antique layers – full of pockets of the sort of eccentricity that Dickens captured so well. There's room in it for tremendous wealth, for brilliant display – but also for squalor, for darkness and menace, for the abuse of the vulnerable and the frail. Things like the possibility of falling from respectability to degradation, the thrills and dangers of 'slumming it' and of living a secret life, the risky excitements of passing oneself off as something one is not: these are all made possible by Victorian city living, so it's no surprise that they should all be such recurrent motifs both in the fiction written by the Victorians themselves and in our own neo-Victorian fantasies. If we want to indulge in a certain kind of narrative – something a bit melodramatic, perhaps – the Victorian city seems to offer us a brilliant template for it.

Are we essentially still living in a Victorian city?

Yes, I think we are, in all sorts of ways. In London, for one thing, we're living in a city that was, in large part, physically constructed by the Victorians: we're still using their Tube system, their sewers, their bridges, and we're still living on streets that were laid down by them, streets that reflect the particular social relations of their era. Think of the difference between the grand streets of the West End, which are all about wealth, leisure and display, and the narrow, crowded, uniform streets of the working-class East. Think of all the imposing buildings of London, with their wonderfully decorated surfaces, which could only have been built at a time when labour was (criminally) cheap. But the gap between wealth and poverty in London is still so acute that – in class terms, at least – it can sometimes seem feel as though the city is still a Dickensian one. We no longer have child labour – that's one improvement – but that's partly because we've pushed the issue overseas. The Victorians lived with child labourers on their streets – perhaps with more honesty than us.

@ **Your queer reworking of the Victorian novel put the 'neo' into neo-Victorianism. How fundamental has queer theory been to the Victorian revivalism of the last fifteen years?**

Well, queer theory's certainly done a lot to make us rethink the Victorians, to explode all those categories and essentialisms of which the Victorians themselves were so fond, to reveal the cracks, doubts, anxieties and panics in nineteenth-century discourses – to make the Victorians, in fact, more complicated, more interesting. But queer theory's been part of a much broader revisionary movement that's included feminist theory, Marxist theory, postcolonial theory... We can't look at the Victorians now without wanting to know what was happening between the classes, what the sexual politics were, how the Empire functioned, who the hidden or voiceless people were. That idea of giving voice to characters who haven't been given voices before, who might have been excluded from the fictions of the nineteenth century, or are misrepresented by them, or are just visible in their margins – that's perhaps been the biggest engine for our form of Victorian revivalism. It isn't a new thing. Jean Rhys did it brilliantly with her *Jane Eyre* retelling *Wide Sargasso Sea*. But it really took off as an idea, I think, in the 1990s.

@ **You have described your novels as 'Victorian pantomime' – is a defining aspect of the neo-Victorian novel a sense of theatricality and playfulness?**

It seems that way, doesn't it? I think this is partly because of what I was talking about just now – the fact that the Victorians seem to offer themselves to us so beautifully in such larger-than-life ways. There are just so many things about the nineteenth century that feel extreme, dramatic: the big dehumanising institutions like workhouses and asylums, the big feats of engineering. Even the garments feel extreme – the corsets, the crinoline cages, the bustles, the stove-pipe hats. The Victorians themselves were clearly aware of this dramatic potential. What else is the fiction of Dickens, of Collins, of Thackeray, but a great relishing of excess? What I was very conscious of, too, when I was writing my novels, was how mythologised the culture felt: I had seen the Victorians represented so many times in films and on TV that the representations seemed to have taken on a life of their own. I wanted to play with that mythology, as much as – perhaps even, more than – I wanted to get close to the Victorians themselves. How can you get close to them, in fact? You can only reinvent them, over and over again. I think that a lot of neo-Victorian fiction understands that, and enjoys it.

You have spoken about the links between your academic background and your writing. Was academia a help or a hindrance when trying to reimagine the Victorian novel – did you feel paralysed by theory?

Well, the sort of academic work I did for my PhD wasn't actually very theory based at all. I looked at lesbian and gay historical literature from the late nineteenth century onwards – I was interested in finding out how queer people had understood and represented themselves and 'their' past, how they'd been understood and represented by mainstream culture; I wanted to know about the actual texture of Victorian queer life. So, no, that work wasn't a hindrance when I came to write fiction; on the contrary, it provided a great springboard for me. And I'd read an awful of Victorian fiction, just for pleasure. I felt very at home on that landscape, very comfortable with its idioms. So the two things came together – that academic grounding in the hints and fragments of lesbian and gay history, and a sense of how to use the Victorian novel form itself to flesh those hints and fragments out.

How do you feel about your novels being studied?

It's funny – when I was a student I used to imagine that being a novelist and having one's work pored over by academics would be just about as thrilling as life could get. Now that I'm a novelist I find the idea of my books being studied oddly unexciting. I think it's because my chief concern as an author is to provide an emotional experience for a reader, and somehow the idea of someone analysing that experience feels all wrong – like explaining a joke. Or maybe it's something about not wanting to revisit my novels. I put years of thought and energy into them while I'm working on them. The thought of someone else doing the same to them after they're finished just makes me feel a bit tired!

Your more recent novels have moved away from a Victorian setting – is there anywhere left for Victorian revivalism to go?

I left the nineteenth century because I felt that, after my 'novel of sensation', *Fingersmith*, I was in danger not just of pastiching the

Victorians but of pastiching myself. But perhaps pastiche is the only way it can go. There's a lot of steampunk around, isn't there? I visited a historical novel writing workshop recently and, while half the class were doing 'straight' historical novels, the other half seemed to be all writing about vampires and elves – putting vampires and elves, I mean, into an actual period landscape. That makes me feel a bit miffed – I have, after all, put a lot of hard work into making my historical settings 'authentic'; what's the point, if you can just make it all up and stick a fairy in? But it also excites me. It's a declaration of what I was talking about earlier – the fact that historical narratives can never be 'authentic'. It's all smoke and mirrors – why not have fun with that?

Was your interest in the nineteenth century purely literary or do you have a fascination for Victorian 'things', such as painting and the decorative arts? Is there anything that you collect?

There is a certain Gothic Victorian quality that has always appealed to me. Even as a child I liked it. Do you remember that *Doctor Who* story from the Tom Baker era, *The Talons of Weng-Chiang*? It's set in a Victorian music hall; there's a scene in which Leela, dressed in Victorian clothes, gets chased through the sewers by a giant rat. That was my favourite *Doctor Who* story, ever. I'm sure bits of it found their way into my first novel, *Tipping the Velvet*. And since then – yes, I've acquired a fair bit of Victoriana. I have quite a big collection of Victorian and Edwardian postcards, which I find just the most compelling and poignant things: they offer us these amazing little windows into ordinary people's lives. And one of my favourite possessions is an engraving from 1901, showing a woman throwing herself off a London bridge into the churning river below, her late-Victorian skirts billowing out behind her. It could be an illustration of the final scene in my second novel, *Affinity* – but I bought it in an antique shop when I was about seventeen, long before I ever thought of writing fiction. It gives me a great thrill to look at that picture and feel a sense of continuity with my younger, Gothic-loving self.

What would be on your Victoriana reading list (this may include actual Victorian as well as neo-Victorian novels)?

Well, as far as neo-Victorian fiction goes, in some ways I'm the worst person to ask for a reading list: almost as soon as I started writing neo-Victorian novels of my own, I ceased being able to read other people's, so I missed out on what I can see from afar are some really terrific recent reimaginings of the period – novels like Michel Faber's *The Crimson Petal and the White* and Jane Harris's *The Observations*. The novels which had a big, direct impact on me are all from the 1990s or earlier: they include *The French Lieutenant's Woman*, *Oscar and Lucinda*, *Possession* and *Nights at the Circus* (by, respectively, John Fowles, Peter Carey, A. S. Byatt and Angela Carter). They are all important novels, not just for me personally, but in wider literary terms, because they did an enormous amount to give historical fiction a sort of literary credibility that, I think, it had lacked a bit before. In particular, they helped to reignite popular interest in the Victorians and in how we think of them.

In terms of critical studies of the period – I'm still thinking of books that had an influence on me personally – Judith Walkowitz's *City of Dreadful Delight* gives a wonderful analysis of various narratives of sexual menace in late-Victorian London, including those surrounding the figure of Jack the Ripper, and Elaine Showalter's *Sexual Anarchy* is brilliant on the moral panics of the same period, and their parallels with the panics of our own. More recently, Kate Summerscale's *The Suspicions of Mr Whicher* offers a gripping, illuminating account of a real-life Victorian murder case. It's a book I'd love to have written myself.

Murder, sex, hysteria… I'm afraid my take on the nineteenth century is hopelessly skewed in favour of the Gothic. But the Victorians were so good at it! My reading list of texts from the period itself would have to include all of Dickens, all of the Brontës, Wilde's *The Picture of Dorian Gray*, Stevenson's *Dr Jekyll and Mr Hyde*, Stoker's *Dracula*, Collins's *The Woman in White* and *Basil*, Le Fanu's *Uncle Silas* and *The Rose and the Key*; it would feature the work on spiritualism, thought-transference and 'phantasms of the living' by writers like Frank Podmore, Fredrick Myers and Edmund Gurney; it would have the eleven-volume sexual autobiography by 'Walter', *My Secret Life*; the bibliographies of erotic literature of Henry Spencer Ashbee; and the diaries of A. J. Munby, who was obsessed with collecting photographs of working women and girls. There must be more wholesome reading than that, though I can't bring any to mind at the moment… Oh, how about Henry Mayhew, whose interviews with ordinary working people in *London Labour and the London Poor* is an absolute essential.

THE VICTORIANS

MATTHEW SWEET

ACH DAY of my working life, I walk home with the Victorians. The train deposits me at the railway station where, in 1877, a dying heiress named Harriet Staunton was carried from the platform by her murderous relations – the opening act of an infamous case known as the Penge Mystery. A few minutes later I pass the street that was once home to W. G. Grace, the greatest cricketer of the age. I pick up my daughters from the after-school club on Jew's Walk, just opposite the house where Eleanor Marx co-ordinated the Bryant and May match-girls' strike and squandered her affections on a conniving boyfriend. The five-minute journey back to our flat takes in a drinking fountain erected in Victoria's honour by a notorious embezzler named Theophilus Williams, the clock-tower of St Bartholomew's Church (committed to canvas by Camille Pissarro in 1871), and the modest house once occupied by August Manns, the conductor who revolutionised British concert-going by persuading audiences to stop talking and actually listen to the music. And this is nothing special: most British suburbs have as dense a population of Victorian ghosts.

What have the Victorians done for us? There's an obvious answer to that question – one that involves sanitation, electricity, railways, cinema, Bovril and Sainsbury's. Let's reframe the question: what have the Victorians done for us lately? The answer to that is more obscure and less edifying, and might require a more complex response than a thin retrospective cheer for Isambard Kingdom Brunel.

I spent the mid-90s working on a DPhil thesis about Wilkie Collins – an experience that left me with the impression that nobody hated the Victorians more than Victorianists. It was a common pursuit. We celebrated inhabitants of the nineteenth century who looked like moderns born before their time, and doled out genteel punishment beatings to the rest. We truffled through the printed record for something called 'Victorian ideology', and when we found it – in medical literature, in forgotten fiction, in yellowed copies of the *Christian Remembrancer* – we brought it to the seminar room and chuckled over it like those robots in the ads for instant mashed potato.

I'd like to claim it was our own idea, but the paper trail went back at least as far as Bloomsbury. For Lytton Strachey and his peers, the Victorians were 'a bunch of mouthing bungling hypocrites'. In a letter to Virginia Woolf, he asked, 'is it prejudice, do you think, that makes us hate the Victorians, or is it the truth of the case?'[1] In the 1940s, Victoria's subjects were patronised by railway-bookstand Freudians, who exposed the 'conscious and unconscious exhibitionism' of women who draped their piano legs for decency's sake – a practice that never took place.[2] In the 1960s, the 'Other Victorians' emerged from Steven Marcus's book of that name – the rebels who wrote about their erotic lives with an 'anti-Victorian effort of honesty'.[3] In the 1970s, the French theorist Michel Foucault pointed out that nineteenth-century reticence was a twentieth-century myth, but instead of using this assertion to liberate the Victorians from the prejudices that had accrued around them, British scholars used Foucault's research to strengthen the case for the prosecution. Throughout the 1980s, they enumerated nineteenth-century barbarities in increasingly shrill terms – which meant that by the time I wandered into the room, it was quite hard to dissent from the view that the Victorian era was a police state of the sensibility.

Since that time, something has shifted. The Victorians are not the people they once were. A decade ago, for instance, Jack the Ripper was the murderous instrument of the nineteenth-century establishment. In *From Hell* (1989–96), he was despatched by Queen Victoria to safeguard humiliating royal secrets with a killing spree – the customary Ripper plotline since *Murder by Decree* (1979). Not anymore. In the TV drama *Ripper Street* (2013), Jack is something much more mundane: a murderer who has proved that police methods are in urgent need of reform. In a 2012 episode of *Doctor Who*, he was an early-evening snack for a crime-fighting lizard called Madame Vastra. 'How did you find him?' asks her wife. 'Stringy', she replies.

For a century Victorian Britain was written up as a kind of prison; slowly, as time passes, it is looking more like a playground. Both ideas say much more about us that they do about the Victorians. The inhabitants of the nineteenth century have provided a bolster for our dubious sense of moral superiority. Now we have asked them to entertain other fantasies, and they are as obliging as only the silent dead can be. And if the Victorians are slowly being relieved of some of their more humiliating duties – as our principal exemplars of sexual hypocrisy and patriarchal badness, for example – that does not necessarily indicate that our culture is treating them more generously. What it really means, I suspect, is that we have reassigned their roles to figures from other periods. In the 1950s and 60s, the nineteenth-century woman was accepted as history's perfect victim: confined by corsetry, misogyny and sexual repression. A younger model has displaced her. Betty Draper from *Mad Men* has done Elizabeth Barrett Browning out of a job.

The Victorians in my neighbourhood are harder to typecast. Harriet Staunton was bullied to death. Eleanor Marx was a political activist who fell in love with a self-serving creep. Theophilus Williams was a local politician with his hand in the till. August Manns loved classical music. No great moral gulf seems to divide their world from ours.

During Victoria's reign, the population of Sydenham rose from 2,800 to 40,000. One or two things have happened here since then. The odd V2 has fallen. A-ha recorded *Take on Me* in what is now the Nisa 7-eleven on Kirkdale. Jason Statham used to live in the flat above the dentist. The neighbourhood, however, remains inescapably Victorian. I like it that way.

---

1 Paul Levy (ed.), *The Letters of Lytton Strachey* (London: Viking, 2005), p. 211.

2 H. Grisewood (ed.), *Ideas and Beliefs of the Victorians* (London: Sylvan Press, 1949), p. 363.

3 Steven Marcus, *The Other Victorians* (New York: Basic Books, 1966), p. 162.

DEMONSTRATIVE DIGITS

CATHERINE FLOOD

Have you ever noticed how often the graphic symbol of a pointing finger pops up to guide you through your day? As you navigate the internet, your cursor arrow changes into a tiny pointing finger every time you hover over a hyperlink. If you visited the Olympic Park during the London 2012 Games the chances are you were waved in the right direction by a marshal wielding a giant demonstrative digit cut out of pink foam.

It is a motif with a long pedigree. From at least the twelfth century, both scribes and their readers drew exquisite pointing hands in the margins of manuscripts in order to draw attention to important passages – a way of taking the text in hand.[1] Like many scribal conventions, the demonstrative digit crossed over into printing practice. Often known as a 'printer's fist' (or simply a 'fist'), it became a wood-engraved or cast-metal block that could be slotted into a letterpress forme alongside the pieces of type. Their design became standardised: an outline of a hand, index finger extended, protruding from a section of sleeve. There are, however, lively variations in the twist of the wrist, the clench of the fist, the elegance of the finger and the style of the cuff – the little differences that encourage connoisseurship.

Although it was in common use much earlier, the printer's fist has a particular resonance with the nineteenth century when it grew in size and flourished in the increasingly competitive environment of bill poster advertising. Here the job of the printer was to take the (often verbose) copy written by the client and lay it out so as to be legible on the street for an audience that was on the move and semi-literate. Along with the use of bold new display fonts, the printer's fist helped attract the eye to the most salient words on the sheet. It functioned somewhere between a directional arrow, an exclamation mark and a decorative ornament. These were days before Modernism and its reverence for white space. The logic of composing a letterpress bill poster was to fill up each line and a printer's fist often provided a handy makeweight.

In recent years Victorianesque printer's fists have been appearing in all kinds of places – dangling from the strings of high-end tea-bags, pointing the way upstairs in a pub that wants to evoke a quirky olde-worlde charm, or a shop that makes some claim to artisan quality (Figs 3.1a–3.1h). To the modern eye, the motif wavers deliciously between the imperious and the absurd. A neatly cuffed printer's fist

AN ALBUM OF
DEMONSTRATIVE DIGITS,
ALL PHOTOGRAPHED OUT
AND ABOUT BY CATHERINE
FLOOD AND NICOLA
SWANN, AUGUST 2012–APRIL
2013, UNLESS OTHERWISE
STATED:

3.1A

3.1B

3.1C

3.1D

(FIG. 3.1A)
NEW NORTH PRESS,
REVERTING TO TYPE (2010).
LETTERPRESS EXHIBITION
POSTER IN BLACK AND RED.
COPYRIGHT THE ARTIST.

(FIG. 3.1B)
AMBIENT ADVERTISING
SIGN ON THE PAVEMENT
OUTSIDE KINGS CROSS
STATION, LONDON.

(FIG. 3.1C)
STEWARD OUTSIDE THE
OLYMPIC PARK DURING
LONDON 2012 GAMES.

(FIG. 3.1D)
SIGNPOST ON KENSINGTON
ROAD, LONDON MADE IN
1911 AND STILL IN SITU.

(FIG. 3.1E)
PACKAGING FOR DR
STUART'S TEA-BAGS.

(FIG. 3.1F)
SIGN ON THE WALL OF
THE CLOTHING SHOP
WHITE STUFF IN SALISBURY
(PRINTER'S FISTS DID NOT
TRADITIONALLY APPEAR
AT AN ANGLE BECAUSE
THEY WERE PRINTED
FROM STANDARD BLOCKS
THAT SAT IN LINE WITH
THE TYPE).

(FIG. 3.1G)
POSTCARD BY CRISPIN
FINN AT THE 2013 PICK
ME UP GRAPHIC ART
FAIR, SOMERSET HOUSE,
LONDON. COPYRIGHT THE
ARTIST.

(FIG. 3.1H)
STEPHEN KENNY, *DISAPPEAR
HERE* (2010). LETTERPRESS
PRINT. COPYRIGHT THE
ARTIST.

3.1E

3.1F

3.1G

3.1H

is a firm, but restrained gesture – there is none of the hyperbole of a propaganda poster with a finger pointing directly at you ('Your Country Needs You'). It seems to speak of a bygone era of etiquette and attention to detail. At the same time, there is an undeniable element of surrealism in a floating, disembodied hand. Contemporary letterpress artist Stephen Kenny (creator of A Two Pipe Problem Press) plays with the enigmatic edge of the printer's fist in his print 'Disappear Here' (Fig. 3.1h). Like a sign for some mysterious fairground magic show it directs the viewer to who knows where.

Today printer's fists are applied knowingly to achieve a fashionable retro aesthetic, but they also signpost a serious revival of interest in the craft of letterpress. The decline of letterpress as a commercial technology has created both a skill vacuum and the possibility for a new kind of creative involvement with the process. While the solid expertise of apprenticeship-trained printers and compositors has been lost, artists and graphic designers have gained the opportunity to experiment with a process from which they were once excluded by the unionisation of the printing trade. The activities of a present day letterpress printer such as Kenny include the production of graphic art for people's walls; exquisite stationery; commissions from advertisers, fashion designers, record labels and museums; a collaborative project with the *Big Issue*; and running workshops for print-curious members of the public who happily get inky for an afternoon.

As a practice, letterpress offers an escape from the daily grind of flat screens. It is the full-bodied experience of a physical process as opposed to fingertips manipulating digital interfaces. It's 'man over mouse' and there are beguiling sensual pleasures: heady turpentine fumes, the sticky hissing noise as you ink up the roller, the smooth touch of wood type polished by years of service, the satisfying mechanical action of a cast-iron Albion press and the subtle kiss of the letters onto quality paper.

It is easy to enter into the period romance of it all, but there is more than nostalgia at play. Letterpress is regaining ground in some colleges of art and design because it teaches timeless skills and principles. It slows down the design process. While a computer executes your commands instantly at the click of a button, every alteration to a letterpress composition is labour intensive and has to be proofed. It is a technique that demands thinking by doing and encourages a reflective and disciplined approach to the work at hand. [2]

Sometimes there is a tendency to accentuate the characteristics of a letterpress print by devices such as under-inking to highlight the imperfections of worn out typefaces, making the impression too deep or mismatching fonts. To some this is an affront to the skills of the past because what we now admire as charming printerly effects were once considered printing mistakes that would have ended up on the workshop floor. Yet undoubtedly part of the allure of letterpress is its status as something handmade with all the connotations of authenticity and sincerity that attach to that. As *Eye Magazine* points out: 'in a time when there is an apparent loss of confidence in the messages of corporations and governments, letterpress seems to speak in a voice we can trust.'[3] There is an urge to reveal the humanity of the technology in the final work. In this context the printer's fist has one more trick up its sleeve – it is a symbol that playfully reminds us of the hidden hand of the printer.[4]

---

1 For the history of the pointing finger symbol see Chapter 2, 'Toward a History of the Manicule', in William H. Sherman, *Used Books: Marking Readers in Renaissance England* (Philadelphia: University of Pennsylvania Press, 2008). See also Charles Hasler, 'A Show of Hands', *Typographica*, 8 (1953), pp. 4–11.

2 For a full discussion of the role of letterpress in graphic design education today, see Alex Cooper, Rosie Gridneff and Andrew Haslam, *6x6: Collaborative Letterpress Project* (forthcoming, 2013).

3 *Eye Blog*, 'Lay out – Speak Out', 20 December 2012. Online: www. eyemagazine.com/blog/post/ lay-out-speak-out. Accessed 7 May 2013.

4 With thanks to the following people for their thoughts on letterpress and the demonstrative digit: Martin Andrews, Graham Bignell, Alex Cooper, Stephen Kenny, Michael Twyman.

NEO-VICTORIAN THINGS: A SCRAPBOOK

SONIA SOLICARI

From glass domes to taxidermy, Staffordshire dogs to flock wallpaper, the past decade has marked the return of the decorative. Many designers, reared on a more pared-down aesthetic, have looked back to those historical moments when greater opportunity for domestic adornment encouraged ornate expression – dado rails anyone? Similarly, contemporary artists have rediscovered 'stuff' – the clutter of objects and patterns that shapes our relationship to the material world. The question of whether a will to decorate and adorn can be sheltered under the umbrella of neo-Victorianism opens up a debate about revivalism that is as frustrating as it is fruitful and suggests the inevitability with which fashion recycles and reworks the visual. From style and taste to political statement and psychological unease – what is real and what is imagined, what is hidden and exposed, in our (re) negotiation of the past?

These questions formed the backdrop to the planning of the exhibition *Victoriana: The Art of Revival* at Guildhall Art Gallery. I do not attempt to provide answers here, but hope that the following snap-shots of neo-Victorianism present an illuminating scrapbook exploring the artistic impulse to look back.

Where better to start our inquisitive browse than with **Mark Titchner**'s seemingly affirmative *I Want a Better World, I Want a Better Me* (Fig. 4.1). Drawing on nineteenth-century trade union banners, the bold design was originally conceived for the 2012 Firstsite exhibition 'News from Nowhere', inspired by William Morris's 1890 utopian–socialist novel of the same name. However, Titchner's interest lies in the tension between Morris's avant-garde politics and the conservative good taste his designs represent today. *I Want a Better World* samples elements of contemporary wallpaper of Morrisian decorative lineage but produced and sold cheaply by multinational companies criticised for poor labour conditions in developing countries.

4.1

William Morris also plays a starring role in **Ligia Bouton**'s graphic-novel inspired, super-designer face-off, *The Adventures of William Morris Man*, which sees the eponymous hero do battle for our homes with *Grammar of Ornament* author Owen Jones (Fig. 4.2). Bouton's intricate explosions of pattern expose the tensions of taste, not only inherent in the nineteenth century itself but in our notion of what it means to be modern, versus the overwhelming Victorian aesthetic legacy.

4.2

4.3

Richard Slee's *Grill* further disrupts notions of decorative design by presenting work which hovers between fine art and functionality (Fig. 4.3). The use of the ornate to frame the practical speaks of the decorative excesses of the past. Ceramic as a medium adds an element of fragility and vulnerability and, alongside other recent works (such as *Switch*, 2010 – an elaborate but unusable device), represents Slee's move 'From Utility to Futility' (exhibition at the V&A, June 2010–

April 2010). *Grill* is what the Victorians could have made – and Slee's characteristic bright yellow pop-art glaze is a simultaneous reproach to, and celebration of, the past.

This sense of the real and the imagined in our relationship to the past is central to the work of **Piers Jamson** whose photographs 'show interior spaces [...] full of tension and redolent of some special but unknowable purpose' (Fig. 4.4).[1] Jamson, who describes his work as 'anti-installation installation' meticulously constructs small-scale interior sets, which are then photographed before being destroyed. The resulting images are both evocative and evasive – a quasi-revivalism that suggests the fallacy of historic sources.

The process of destruction central to Jamson's work raises questions about the preservation of the past and the creation of the future. Most of us still live with the Victorians in our homes and cities – private places and public spaces that staged the hopes and fears of a now 'lost', unknowable, civilisation that has left its spectral trace. The walls of our inhabited spaces are papered with **Timorous Beasties'** *Devil Damask Flock* with its ghostly impression of shapes and faces, as unnerving as it is historically comforting (and used to great effect in the bedroom of femme fatale Irene Adler in the neo-Victorian television drama *Sherlock*) (Fig. 4.5).

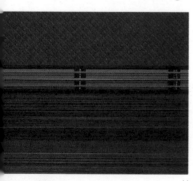

4.4

These decorative phantoms haunt **Jake and Dinos Chapman**'s 'Family Portrait' series, an ongoing project for which the artists source unwanted nineteenth-century portraits, which they then alter to create macabre images of forgotten ancestors (Fig. 4.6). Their work destabilises the notion of 'passing down'; certainly, the way that we acquire, re-use and re-situate objects lies at the heart of neo-Victorian anxiety and the simultaneous fascination and discomfort with the

aesthetic of revivalism itself. It also forms the inspiration behind armchair destructivist **Miss Pokeno**'s *Trophy Chair*, in which the practical tweed and velvet frontage belies the knotted back of taxidermic vulpinity (Fig. 4.7). For Pokeno, the chair confronts the decorative oppression but strange allure of England – still 'Victorian' to her New Zealand childhood impressions, but now ripe for confrontation.

The resurgence of taxidermy marks an engagement with survival and preservation but also presents a perceived rectification of a social oversensitivity to death and dignity. As 'fine-art taxidermist' Polly Morgan suggests, 'people are coming to their senses, post-political correctness, and rediscovering the beauty of what the world is all about'.[2] Works such as Pokeno's and Morgan's, which use animals that have died 'natural and unpreventable' deaths, are both quietly poetic and unavoidably challenging – reviving, as they do, one of the more extreme aesthetics of the nineteenth century. They also reconcile the simultaneous cruelty and sentiment of the Victorians with our own ethical questions around the passing of life and times.

4.6   4.7

This complication of beauty underpins the imagined worlds of **Tessa Farmer**. Her insect tableaux are inspired by Victorian illustrator Richard Doyle's fairies – attacking and goading, carousing and cajoling (Fig. 4.8). Nonetheless, her 'tiny spectacles […] evolve as something alien and futuristic' suggesting the enduring fascination of the natural world made artificial but also the meticulous mind of the Victorian collector.[3] Similarly, **Patrick StPaul**'s *Whisper In The*

NEO-VICTORIAN THINGS

Midst Of Silence, which the artist describes as 'life, the universe and everything, in a glass cabinet', operates in the chasm between memory and its embodiment in objects, taking inspiration from an idea of collecting that is essentially Victorian and taxonomic (Fig. 4.9).[4] *Whisper* also plays on our simultaneous fascination and revulsion with the medical and the relationship between art and science, as embodied by the nineteenth-century cabinet.

4.8

4.9

In terms of a discernible neo-Victorian aesthetic, the revival of the collector has led the way in the return of the now ubiquitous glass dome as a means of showcasing a work of art. Much has been written about the original Victorian fascination with the 'artificial kingdom' and the use of glass to create a staged hyper-reality.[5] Certainly, vitrines as proto-postmodernist signifiers already credit the Victorians with a kitsch significance that revivalism would find hard to reclaim. The current vogue for such an effective means of object veneration merely marks a more self-conscious positioning of the consumer as artist/curator. When employed, such exhibits become neo-Victorian super-tools, enabling the individual to bell-jar their personality – combining wit with a mastery of historic display. It is perhaps under the glass dome that neo-Victorianism will eventually eat itself.

This preoccupation with the artificial kingdom is central to the work of **Chantal Powell**, whose use of fake flowers 'inhabit(s) a place that is somewhere between wonder and disappointment'.[6] Powell's *Siren*, for example, encages blooms in a Paxton-esque architectural structure – threatening to escape from the skeleton of a neo-Victorian framing device and a notion of oppressive nineteenth-century industrialisation (Fig. 4.10). **Jane Hoodless**'s *Pteridomania* series, inspired by the nineteenth-century craze for ferns, also speaks of the Victorian preoccupation with collecting and encasing (Fig. 4.11). Her paper Wardian cases are themselves imitations of an imitation of nature. For Hoodless, the fern motif has added resonance for its popularity in Victorian decorative design and her work thus traces the patterns of the past.

4.10

4.11

Neo-Victorian things carry with them the 'memory' of display. Whether or not they are now situated against the sparse backdrops of the modern interior, they 'remember' the Victorian parlour resplendent with ornaments. The contemporary reclaiming of the Victorian Staffordshire ceramic figure suggests a similar importation of the past into the present through a strong aesthetic signifier. They mark the return of the ornament to the home and the return of the hearth as a focus of domestic decoration. As artist-designed pieces, these reinterpretations also place a layer of individuality onto an historically industrial aesthetic, furthering the new preoccupation with the handmade in the face of mass production.

4.13

4.12

Rob Ryan's *Your Job Is To Take This World Apart And Put It Back Together – But Even Better!!!* is a series of ceramic dogs and cats, based on original moulds but decorated with upbeat slogans and paper-cut designs (Fig. 4.12). Despite their nostalgic appearance, Ryan's ceramics explore an industrial past that is aesthetically unloved and, like the portraits found by the Chapman brothers, free for the taking. Similarly, ceramicist **Carole Windham** uses the established aesthetic framework of the Staffordshire figure to explore contemporary thought and political commentary. *Dearly Beloved* situates David Cameron and Nick Clegg as Queen and Consort in a commemoration of their policies on gay marriage (Fig. 4.13).

Windham further challenges our comfort with the aesthetic by playing with the notion of scale. *Dearly Beloved* is sixty-three centimetres high, much taller than the Victorian ceramics on which it is based, questioning both our familiarity with recognisable objects and the very idea of the mantelpiece on which they were designed to sit. These are ideas too large for the domestic environment. Indeed, the Staffordshire figure as contemporary political conduit is further played out in the work of **Mathew Weir**. His oil paintings conjure a lurid, almost psychedelic world in which to stage renderings of original Victorian ceramics, such as the recurring figure of American abolitionist John Brown. The artificiality of the still life made modern challenges any residual sentimentalisation of the past through exploration of the uncomfortable socio-political climate of imperialism, racism and child exploitation in which the Victorians operated (Fig. 4.14).

Such works at once blow apart and celebrate our new-found love of Victorian things, exposing both shame and pride in our historic legacy. They also raise the question of nostalgia in our love of the past – a notion which comes crashing to the floor in ceramicist **Barnaby Barford**'s film *Damaged Goods,* set in the Victoriana world of a bric-a-brac shop and telling a tragic love story through porcelain figurines – many of which are themselves twentieth-century reworkings of eighteenth- and nineteenth-century ceramics (Fig. 4.15).

(FIG. 4.14 OPPOSITE)
MATHEW WEIR, *HANGMAN* (2010). OIL ON CANVAS, MOUNTED ON BOARD. COPYRIGHT THE ARTIST. IMAGE COURTESY OF THE ALISON JACQUES GALLERY.

(FIG. 4.15)
BARNABY BARFORD, *DAMAGED GOODS* (2008). FILM STILL. COPYRIGHT THE ARTIST.

4.15

The need to both venerate and destroy the past is given similarly surreal creative vent in **Tom Werber**'s video animation for Losers' *Flush* – a song about the purging of a failed relationship.[7] Using **Dan Hillier**'s altered engravings, via Max Ernst's fantasy collages of the 1920s and 30s, the animation begins in a Victorian home (Fig. 4.16). Eventually, the dysfunctional couple tear through the walls in their struggle to free themselves from domestic tension, before embarking on a destructive stomp through a reimagined Victorian London. The juxtaposition of contemporary music with Victorian-inspired animation immediately locates and exploits the post-punk potential of the nineteenth-century aesthetic – a buttoned-up Britishness ripe for reclamation and defamation but with an undercurrent of aggressive affection. The frenetic imagination of Werber's work also suggests the creativity which stems from our inability to really understand and capture the Victorian past – an embrace of unsettled historical identity.

4.16

Certainly, the enduring notion of Victorian identity has formed the message of many artistic reworkings of recent years. Who can forget Nick Knight's iconic image of Aimee Mullins, part of a fashion story art directed by Alexander McQueen for *Dazed & Confused* magazine in 1998. The model, who wears antiqued prosthetic legs and is encapsulated by a crinoline petticoat – appropriates the language of Victoriana. However, the modern lens turns inherited perceptions of femininity and disability into a groundbreaking commercial image that challenges assumptions about physical beauty.

In this vein, **Phil Sayers**' *Shalott* (after J. W. Waterhouse's 1894 oil *The Lady of Shalott*) repositions Tennyson's heroine in a post-feminist world that at once recognises and rejects the historical positioning of women and feminity. Sayers' transvestite vision adopts the Victorian in order to stage a debate around the role of sex and gender in contemporary society (Fig. 4.17). The Lady in Sayers' reimagining emerges from a tangle of cables and wires which symbolise the 'things' which bind and control the modern world and suggest our cultural transition from real space to cyberspace.

Such images strike at the heart of our enduring fascination with the Victorian – a monolithic but ultimately impenetrable age. Cultured but cruel, enlightened but oppressive, technologically progressive but socially regressive – the Victorians are all and none of these things. Their evasion of definition presents not so much a blank canvas as a chaotic collage that can be worked and reworked by artist and public. Neo-Victorian things, real and imagined, created and curated, are our attempt to find meaning in the physical world. They suggest an unfurnished room waiting to be decorated with the hopes and fears which surround our negotiation of contemporary identity through aesthetic legacy. They also offer an aesthetic rebellion against streamlined design, minimalist interiors and modern understandings of good taste. Most of all, they speak about us – our past, our present and our future, as negotiated through the things we buy and sell, create and destroy, love and loathe, cut out and keep.

1 David Lillington, Press Release for Piers Jamson, *Empire View*, Elevator Gallery, 11 May 2012–3 June 2012. Online: www.elevatorgallery.co.uk/wp-content/uploads/2012/02/ELEVATOR-PRESS-RELEASE.pdf. Accessed 1 June 2012.

2 Polly Morgan, in Joanna Bale, 'Back from the dead to liven up your sitting room', *The Times* (11 November 2006). Online: www.thetimes.co.uk/tto/news/uk/article1942768.ece. Accessed 1 June 2012.

3 Patricia Ellis, 'About Tessa' (2007). Online: www.tessafarmer.com. Accessed 1 April 2013.

4 Patrick StPaul's website. Online: www.patrickstpaul.com/portfolio.html. Accessed 1 April 2013.

5 See Celeste Olalquiaga, *The Artificial Kingdom: A Treasury of the Kitsch Experience* (London: Bloomsbury, 1998).

6 Chantal Powell, 'Exploring a Key Material in my Practice – Artificial Flowers'. Online: http://chantalpowell.wordpress.com/2012/02/13/exploring-a-key-material-in-my-practice-artificial-flowers. Accessed 1 April 2013.

7 Music video for Losers, *Flush feat. Riz MC & Envy* (2010). Dir. Tom Werber; artwork Dan Hillier. Online: www.youtube.com/watch?v=dsaLyUTDGTo. Accessed 11 May 2013.

4.17

T IS FOR

TERMINAL
VELOCIPEDE

THE LOST PROPERTY

LEE JACKSON

LTHOUGH she was a confident and self-possessed young woman, Emily Markham had begun to doubt herself. For she had reached the ripe old age of twenty-five years without finding a husband. With each passing day, she felt her hope ebbing away, her prospects in life diminishing. She had to face the brutal truth. She was in danger of becoming – she could hardly bring herself to contemplate the word – a spinster.

Her failure was not for want of application. Encouraged by her parents, she had equipped herself with all the womanly graces: she wrote with an elegant hand; had mastered point lace-work; made a diligent study of the piano forte; memorised the maidservant's routine (so as to instruct any future Eliza or Mary-Anne that might be placed in her tender care). She had even taken time to acquire a few more unconventional accomplishments. Indeed, her knowledge of taxidermy – with particular reference to the musculature and natural postures of various species of semi-aquatic rodents – was something of a talking point in the local district; and her *tableau des rats d'eau* took pride of place amongst the household gods ranged on the family's mantelpiece. She had all this and more to offer a suitable young man. Nonetheless, likely candidates seemed to fall by the wayside. Several distant cousins had appeared good prospects, then made themselves scarce; likewise, two separate and distinct members of the parish choral society. There was even, at one point, a soldierly gentleman with a considerable pension, due to valuable services rendered at the Battle of Inkerman. Yet all of them beat a retreat when confronted with the reality of Miss Markham.

It was really quite trying.

Miss Markham pondered her failure; but, despite her keen intelligence, she could not intuit the truth – that she had become, if anything, *too* accomplished; there was almost nothing in her which a husband might complement or perfect. Moreover, the brisk and practical manner which aided her immensely in the cause of self-improvement was a hindrance in affairs of the heart. Indeed, her manner was brusque. If she received flowers, she merely placed them in a vase; if she discovered a Valentine on the mat, she filed it amongst her correspondence. In short, she was a practical creature, lacking any serious capacity for romantic sentiment – the sort that most flatters male pride – the very thing she most needed.

Miss Markham, of course, saw none of this.

She was still thinking on the matter one Saturday morning, when she was obliged to take the railway to Nunhead to visit her cousin Evangelina. She sat next to the window, gazing at the rooftops of south London. Now and then, reflections in the glass let her steal surreptitious glances at the men in her compartment. None of the ghostly apparitions were remotely suitable. Too old; too bald; too fond of tobacco. In any case, what was the use? She was no coquette; she possessed no wiles to snare a passing stranger; such things could not be studied – at least, not in respectable society.

'Nun'ed!' shouted the guard.

Miss Markham jumped in astonishment. She had almost missed her stop. She flung open the door and squeezed her crinoline through its narrow confines.

It was only when the train departed that she realised she had left her reticule in the carriage.

The following day, Miss Markham went in search of the Lost Property Office at London Bridge Station. It proved to be a small, smoky little place, next to the Ladies' Waiting Room; and she was obliged to wait several minutes whilst an elderly gentleman remonstrated with the attendant. Finally, she took her place at the counter and spoke to the young official, describing the bag and its embroidery with admirable concision. The uniformed young man, pleasant and deferential, smiled, and went to look for the item in question.

It was only later that evening, sitting in her bedroom, brushing her hair, that her thoughts returned to the station. The young man in the Lost Property Office had smiled at her. Of course, it was nothing. Yet she recalled his face perfectly – rather handsome, as it happened – and his voice. It was quite plain that he was well educated; and *such* an agreeable manner. Idly, she compared and contrasted him with her cousins and the various lions of the choral society, and she immediately concluded that he excelled them in almost every regard.

It was a shame he was a railwayman.

As she lay in bed, she pondered the sort of man she would like to marry. She had always hoped for a superior sort of tradesman, or a well-to-do City clerk. She wondered if the young man at London Bridge had good prospects. By the time she fell asleep, she was quite certain of it.

The following morning, as she buttered her toast, Miss Markham formulated a plan.

It was not difficult to contrive more visits to her cousin in Nunhead; and no one guessed their true purpose.

She began her campaign with the second volume of a novel she had borrowed from Mudie's, carefully abandoned on the 11.15.

On the subsequent visit to the Lost Property Office, she satisfied herself that the young man was not already married – a source of great anxiety – and that he was quite as handsome as she had remembered.

A week later, she made sure her jade brooch came loose on the 12.30 back to London Bridge.

On that visit, she thanked the young man for his helpfulness, and learned that his name was Mr. Prince. The office was quiet, so she asked his opinion on the American war. From his reply, she concluded that he possessed a lively and independent mind, and that she should not want for intelligent conversation. She also noted, with some satisfaction, that he smiled at her again.

The following week, she happened to lose a tract by Mr. Spurgeon on the 10.32.

She made sure to ask the young man if he was a churchgoer.

Three more visits to the Lost Property Office followed, during which Miss Markham reclaimed her best hat, a needlework sampler of particularly exquisite workmanship, and a small volume of Byron's poetry. Her brief moments with the young Mr. Prince became the high point of her week.

Yet – somehow – impossibly – he had made no advance to her. There was no hint of dawning affection; no suggestion of greater intimacy between them.

She resolved to make one final push. After an acquaintance of Evangelina expressed a modest interest in the famous *tableau*, Miss Markham proposed to transport it to Nunhead, allegedly for the purpose of exhibition. The *rats d'eau*, however, never completed the journey, left in a cardboard box on the 9.58.

Miss Markham visited the Lost Property Office feeling tremulous and agitated. She made sure to open the box – as if to check its contents – and that young man seemed suitably impressed. She spoke with modesty of her abilities, and remarked that she would actually prefer to do less indoors, and take more exercise – if only someone might accompany her to the park – or even the theatre –

The young man smiled, nodded, and called for his next customer. Miss Markham, utterly dejected, reclaimed her box and left.

That night, Emily Markham wept bitter tears of regret.

Mr. Edward Prince, on the other hand, sat in a corner of the Butcher's Arms and shared a cheerful drop or two with his pals.

He told them a story about a young woman he had met in the Lost Property Office – a proper stunner – at one point he had even thought of walking out with her.

Oh, my Lord, but so damn forgetful!

No, he could not stand that. He wanted a wife with an ounce of common sense.

O

—IS FOR—
OMNISOMNOAMBULISTS

A NEO-VICTORIAN
ALPHABET

OTTO VON BEACH

—IS FOR—
ANTEPENULTIMATE

B

—IS FOR—
BACHELOR,
CONFIRMED

D

—IS FOR—
DR LIVINGSTONE,
I PRESUME

—IS FOR—
EXPERIMENTS
OF A
REGRETTABLE
NATURE

—IS FOR—
FALLEN WOMEN,
AND THOSE WHO WOULD
PICK THEM UP

—IS FOR—
GIMLET EYE

—IS FOR—
HANDSOME
LEXICOGRAPHERS

—IS FOR—
JUST DESSERTS

—IS FOR—
KEEPSAKE

L

—IS FOR—
LOVE THAT DARE
NOT SPEAK ITS
NAME

M

—IS FOR—
MISSIONARY
POSITION

TROPICAL TUB-THUMPER

Full-time ££neg

TRADITIONAL HEATHEN VILLAGE
SEEKS PERIPATETIC PROSELYTISER

WOULD SUIT CONFIDENT
SELF-STARTER WITH GOOD
EXCOMMUNICATION
SKILLS

Apply to : S.S. Heart of Darkness,
Portsmouth Docks

N

—IS FOR—
NOT CRICKET

P

—IS FOR—
POGONOLOGIST

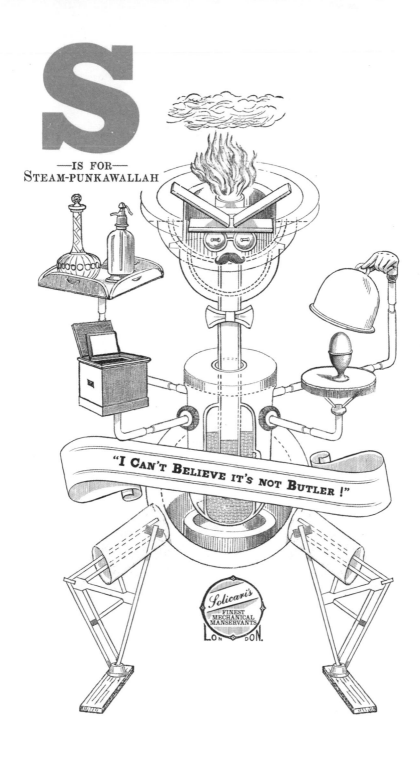

S

—IS FOR—
STEAM-PUNKAWALLAH

"I CAN'T BELIEVE IT'S NOT BUTLER!"

Solicari's
FINEST
MECHANICAL
MANSERVANTS
LONDON.

Q

—IS FOR—
QUIET CONTEMPLATION
OF OUR NATIONAL
ACHIEVEMENTS

W

—IS FOR—
WOMEN ON THE
VERGE OF A
NERVOUS
DISPOSITION

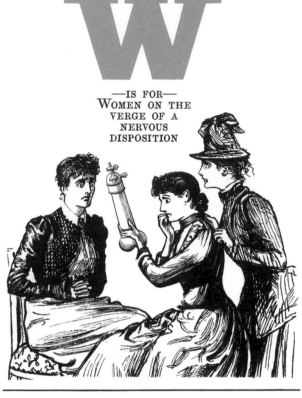

U

—IS FOR—
UPPER LIP,
STIFF

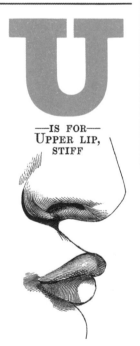

X

—IS FOR—
MULTIPLICATION

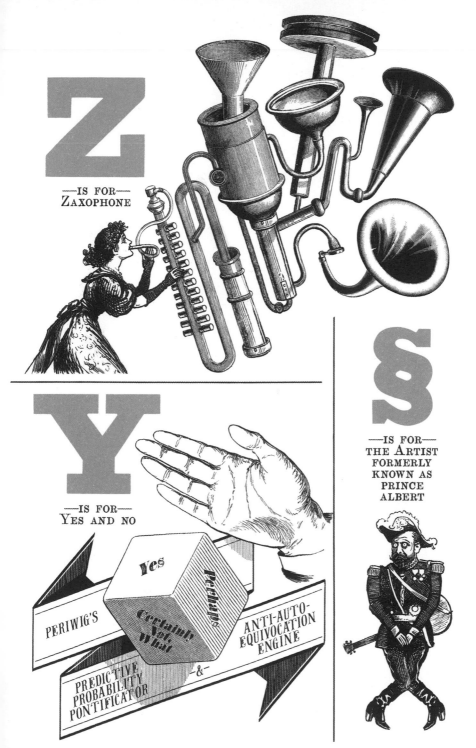

Z

—IS FOR—
ZAXOPHONE

Y

—IS FOR—
YES AND NO

PERIWIG'S

Yes

Perhaps

Certainly Not What

ANTI-AUTO-
EQUIVOCATION
ENGINE

PREDICTIVE
PROBABILITY
PONTIFICATOR

—&—

§

—IS FOR—
THE ARTIST
FORMERLY
KNOWN AS
PRINCE
ALBERT

Otto Von Beach illustrations supported
by the Friends of Guildhall Art Gallery,
Vivien Knight Fund.

STEAMPUNK

KATTY PEARCE

The past is a kind of future that has already happened.[1]

You already know what steampunk is. At least, you probably already know what it looks like. You may not go in for nineteenth-century science fiction. You may not dream of captaining a pirate airship, or consider an aviator helmet and engineer goggles to be acceptable daywear. You may even live without a clockwork octopus in a tank. If you can call that living. Despite these deprivations, whether you realise it or not, the chances are you have already been exposed to the fantasy world of Victorian-inspired contraptions and Mad Inventor chic (Figs 5.1 & 5.2).

(FIG. 5.1)
JOHN COULTHART,
STEAMPUNK (2008). TEXT
BY JEFF VANDERMEER.
VECTOR ART. COPYRIGHT
THE ARTIST.

(FIG. 5.2)
AUTHOR G. D. FALKSEN
SHOWN WITH
MECHANICAL ARM
CREATED BY THOMAS
WILLEFORD. PHOTOGRAPH
BY TYRUS FLYNN.

5.1   5.2

A fantasy genre, a design aesthetic, and for some an entire cultural movement, steampunk has been moving inexorably towards you with whirring cogs and cranking gears, pumping out unwholesome vapours for decades. Industrial and mechanical, it is also paradoxically organic and evolving. Its tentacles have slithered from literary origins to embrace fashion, arts and crafts, interior design, music, engineering and gadgetry.

If you saw the film *Wild Wild West* (1999, based on a 1969 US television series), or the latest incarnation of *Sherlock Holmes* (2010); if you read Alan Moore's series of graphic novels *The League of*

Extraordinary Gentlemen, or even Philip Pullman's *His Dark Materials* trilogy, you already recognise steampunk tropes. Within the last few years, you've seen steampunk style approximated by the catwalk collections of Alexander McQueen, Vivienne Westwood, and Prada; faux-antique fob-watches, double-breasted greatcoats, and buckle-and-strap leather boots have filtered accordingly into the high street. You saw it at the 2012 Olympics opening ceremony, and at the Paralympics closing ceremony, where it was momentarily adopted as the British national aesthetic. Through the haze, begoggled and leather-aproned outsiders regarded you as though you, in your skinny jeans, were the anachronism.

Steampunk is what happens when goths discover brown.[2]

The term 'steampunk' was first coined by sci-fi author K. W. Jeter in 1987 to describe a type of speculative fiction inspired by Victorian-era aesthetics and technology. The word playfully alludes to cyberpunk, a late-twentieth-century genre of postmodern sci-fi that depicts technological dystopian futures (think *Blade Runner*). But where cyberpunk explores nightmare visions of virtual reality and sinister artificial intelligence in possible future worlds, steampunk reimagines the pre-electronic past from the perspective of the future. In common with all strands of science fiction and alternative history, the genre poses the question: What If? Some typical steampunk What Ifs might include:

What if?

∞

*The Victorians had used steam power
to start a space race?*

∞

*Clockwork automatons
began replacing domestic servants?*

∞

*Charles Babbage had succeeded in building
his prototype 'Analytical Engine'
(a mechanical computer) in the 1840s?*

∞

*Hot-air balloons had developed
into the most common mode of transport*

∞

*Steam-powered cars had prevailed
over the internal combustion engine?*

These questions lead to very creative, eccentric and, let's not forget, entertaining answers. In the alternate steam universe antiquated contraptions are cutting-edge, and today's cutting-edge technologies are antiquated. Object makers render twenty-first-century gadgets as though they had been invented 150 years ago – wooden iPhone cases with inbuilt clockwork, modified Qwerty keyboards in mahogany and artificially tarnished brass.

By deviating from the established facts of the past, steampunk remakes the present in a new image. But as anyone who went to the cinema in the 1980s knows, you can't mess with the past without affecting the future. If you follow the technological roads not taken in the nineteenth century, signposted by What Ifs, you arrive at a different kind of future: a retro-future. Because the present is really not all it's cracked up to be.

Steampunk isn't really concerned with recreating or appropriating nostalgic history, nor with investigating specific Victorian events to give voice to untold stories from the past. The ingredients of steampunk may be neo-Victorian in flavour, but they are whipped up into avant-garde recipes, some of which leave a bitter aftertaste.

We are secretly preparing ourselves for the death of our own tech.[3]

———————◆◆◆◆◆———————

The Victorians had their own What Ifs, expressing anxiety about the consequences of industrial progress in some of the earliest examples of speculative fiction (or 'Scientific Romance'). The novels of Jules Verne and H. G. Wells are major inspirations for steampunk, featuring unrealised (but plausibly described) devices: the sea monster-shaped 'Nautilus' submarine in Verne's *Twenty Thousand Leagues Under the Sea* (1870); Wells's *Time Machine* (1895). Their adventure stories are not mere flights of fancy, but explorations of serious ethical questions about imperialism and the pitfalls of overweening ego. Steampunk mines these cautionary tales from the past to fuel similar critique in the present, and challenge our own sense of scientific superiority.

The Industrial Revolution gave us a century built from iron and powered by steam – changing transport, communication, manufacturing and infrastructure. And then we carried on changing it.

So if the Age of Steam seems anachronistic to us today, what might the Digital Age seem like to our descendants? Future generations will surely view our soon-to-be-outdated (if not already dead) devices through retrogoggles. Can we really believe that the tablet computer, or even the internet, will last? 'Tablet computer' – 'Microchip' – 'Gramophone'. When the 4D printer becomes obsolete – what next?

Things are a lot more like they used to be than they are now.[4]

If you ever feel overwhelmed by disappointment at the mass commercial naffness of 'today', you can understand where steampunks are coming from. All that shiny, ticking, whirring paraphernalia, all that burgeoning imaginative promise in the nineteenth century, and what did we, the children of the twentieth century, actually get? Breeze-blocks, hatchbacks and beige shell suits. You might well long to replace plastic and concrete with polished oak and brass. You too might prefer to own one unique, handmade silk corset instead of a million disposable polyester vests, exact copies of which are being disposed of by millions of polyester-vest-wearers every day.

The Victorian backlash against mechanised production methods resulted in the Arts and Crafts movement, harking back to a medieval tradition of handmade objects. Steampunk makers echo their forebears' desire to reclaim historical materials (ironically, those of the Victorian industrial past) to offer a corrective for twenty-first-century blandness. They redesign clothes, accessories, furniture into more satisfying, sexier shapes. They put the romance of the ornamental curio back into functional objects.

Perhaps it is the desire for escapist fantasy which motivates the counter-response to disposable culture. It is also anger in its most creative and whimsical form. For what better way to kick against the aesthetic (and philosophical) horrors of the last forty years – that period of de-industrialisation and plasticisation – than to show it as the aberration it really is? Let's not simply pretend it never happened. Let's replace it entirely. Let's jump timelines and continue on from somewhere different.

If you generate enough steam, you can't see all that polystyrene packaging and nylon underwear. If you fly your giant dirigible high enough, a landscape of phallic glass shards and grey urban brutalism recedes away beneath you.

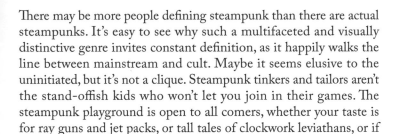

There may be more people defining steampunk than there are actual steampunks. It's easy to see why such a multifaceted and visually distinctive genre invites constant definition, as it happily walks the line between mainstream and cult. Maybe it seems elusive to the uninitiated, but it's not a clique. Steampunk tinkers and tailors aren't the stand-offish kids who won't let you join in their games. The steampunk playground is open to all comers, whether your taste is for ray guns and jet packs, or tall tales of clockwork leviathans, or if you just have a fetish for brown leather.

For those who like their subcultures to remain sub, the gradual breakthrough of steampunk into general public consciousness could be somewhat dismaying. Perhaps it's the sad fate of all punk to go pop. If the word is mentioned in the national press or on daytime TV, it's usually in inverted commas under the 'so what is [insert name of latest trend/internet meme here]?' brand of reporting. Don't panic. Steampunk is resilient and irreverent enough to handle trivial side-glances or serious enquiry, and treat those two impostors just the same.

We can all acknowledge the familiar points of historical reference within the steampunk movement, whilst admiring the beautiful, strange new forms of creative expression which result from the real passion and skill of its practitioners.

Steampunk isn't going anywhere. Except backwards into the future.

---

1 Bruce Sterling, 'The User's Guide to Steampunk', in Jeff VanderMeer, with S. J. Chambers, *The Steampunk Bible* (New York: Abrams, 2011), p. 13.

2 Regularly cited quote attributed to steampunk author Jess Nevins.

3 Sterling, 'User's Guide to Steampunk', p. 13.

4 A catchy slogan on www. steampunkvehicles.tumblr.com.

THE GRAPHIC
NOVEL

TIM KILLICK

The opening of Volume I of *The League of Extraordinary Gentlemen* treats the reader to a graphic version of what Hollywood calls 'the reveal shot'. The first page of the work gives us the date and location for our scene: 'Dover. May, 1898'. The genre can be surmised: the pictorial epigram which forms the preceding frontispiece makes reference to British Intelligence; the waiting man's casual appraisal of the approaching carriage in the mirrored interior of his cigarette case is classic spy tradecraft; the 'John Bull' matchbox and the white cliffs reinforce the impression of England and its defenders. A woman steps from the cab and addresses the man as 'Mr. Bond', but this is Campion, not James – familiar, yet different. She, we are told, is Wilhelmina Murray – wife of the unfortunate Jonathan Harker in Bram Stoker's *Dracula*, and the unwilling recipient of the count's embraces.

So far, so intriguing. As the reader turns the page to the title-panel they get the reveal: the full context of this first encounter (Fig. 6.1). The two characters are reduced to specks atop a vast, half-built structure. This is Albion Reach – a Victoriana fantasy causeway, in the process of being constructed by chugging robo-cranes and featuring a gigantic stone lion and a one-armed Britannia. The cliffs remain just visible in the background, dwarfed in comparison to the man-made monstrosity, which looms proprietorially out across the English Channel. *The League of Extraordinary Gentlemen*, whose first volume appeared in 1999, written by Alan Moore and illustrated by Kevin O'Neill, is perhaps the prototypical neo-Victorian graphic novel. The 'league' in question is a band of literary superheroes transplanted from the pages of romance, gothic and science fiction novels to save the British Empire, and its opening *coup de théâtre* provides one of the best introductions to the tropes and conventions of this particular sub-genre of graphic fiction.

Neo-Victorian graphic novels make the nineteenth century speak to the modern reader by showing us the past in a way that simultaneously critiques the follies and foibles of history and reveals its troubling parallels with the present. Moore's *League* series is part of an increasingly significant comic-book trend, which includes works such as the same author's *From Hell* (illustrated by Eddie Campbell, 1989–96), Warren Ellis and Gianluca Pagliarani's *Aetheric Mechanics* (2008), Bryan Talbot's *Grandville* series (2009–12), Ian Edginton and Davide Fabbri's *The Victorian Undead* (2010), and a host of other titles that depict, evoke or otherwise draw on the

6.1

THE GRAPHIC NOVEL

texture of the nineteenth century. Even the costumed superheroes of DC and Marvel have had their neo-Victorian adventures: Batman in *Gotham by Gaslight* (1989), Superman and other members of the Justice League in *JLA: Age of Wonder* (2003), the X-Men in *Apocalypse vs. Dracula* (2006), just for starters. This is a fundamentally modern cultural phenomenon, steeped in the steampunk fascination with Victorian aesthetics and technology that emerged in the 1980s, but the roots of this retro-futurism stretch much further back – all the way to the nineteenth century itself, and the visions of futurity that swirl through the worlds created by writers from Mary Shelley to H. G. Wells.

(FIG. 6.1)
ALAN MOORE AND KEVIN
O'NEILL, *THE LEAGUE
OF EXTRAORDINARY
GENTLEMEN, VOLUME I*
(LONDON: TITAN, C.2000),
TITLE-PANEL TO ISSUE 1.
IMAGE COURTESY OF TITAN.

A very special combination of word and image is offered by the graphic novel: one which lends itself well to neo-Victorianism. Moore and O'Neill's *League* series not only echoes the visual style of the nineteenth-century illustrated press – ubiquitous from the mid-century, from the *Illustrated London News* to *Punch* – but the writing also riffs on the phraseology of nineteenth-century fiction. Characters variously mimic and subvert the verbal formalities of the novel of the period; similarly, the concluding panels to each issue ape the hyperbole of Victorian juvenile magazines and cheap popular fiction, exhorting the reader to 'reserve the next edition of our illustrated chap-book, and thus learn the outcome of this rousing and invigorating narrative!' Since words and pictures are presented to the reader/viewer simultaneously, the pages of graphic novels are read multicursally (switching between visual and verbal 'texts'). The reader can scan the page, getting the drift of events, and then delve into the details, or they can take in the story panel-by-panel, fitting together speech and action – though this painstaking approach may be deliberately destabilised by the writer and illustrator.

Graphic novels also occupy a peculiar realist position. They are a primarily visual medium, in the sense that the pictures are usually seen before the words are read, and an image is often left to stand alone on a page for maximum impact; however, like all rules, this one can be broken, and graphic novels are equally capable of allowing their imagery to fade into the background while the text takes centre stage. For the most part, graphic novels are representative and realist, but they are not always realistic – nor do they claim to be so. Instead, a suspension of reality is in operation. They possess an inherently metafictional quality, and are exceptionally capable of drawing attention to their own processes: questioning the nature of representation and narrative, and the interplay between the two. Neo-Victorian graphic novels may make reference to actual historical periods, events and figures, but they are not histories, and they can also be intensely self-reflective: interrogating their own structure, composition, referentiality and bias.

One effect of this insistent intertexuality is that graphic novels have an extraordinary scope for presenting alternatives to reality: most enthusiastically embraced by neo-Victorian writers in the form of the counter-factual history. In the world of *The League of Extraordinary Gentlemen*, British colonialism has progressed along broadly historical lines, but the Empire has been assisted by fantastically elaborate technologies, and is populated by people sprung from works of fiction – for the most part by writers roughly contemporaneous to the Victoriana of Volumes I and II (H. G. Wells, Jules Verne, H. Rider Haggard, Arthur Conan Doyle), but often from much further afield (Shakespeare, Ian Fleming, Bertolt Brecht, Iain Sinclair).

In a similar vein, Bryan Talbot's *Grandville* series is set in a twenty-first century that looks like the *belle époch* Paris of the 1890s. In this reality, the Napoleonic Wars were won by France, and Britain consequently became a French colony, only recently emerging as an independent state after a terrorist bombing campaign. To add to the strangeness, most of the characters in *Grandville* are also animals – the hero is a particularly buff badger detective called LeBrock. Talbot's menagerie evokes the anthropomorphic taxidermy of the Victorian period, and is also a nod towards the exploration of humanity's animalistic impulses explored by Stevenson through Jekyll and Hyde, and by Wells through the vivisections of Dr Moreau. Primarily, however, *Grandville's* cartoonish beasts are a visually arresting way of emphasising the otherness of this alternate world – one that, like Moore's, is the same as ours, and very different.

'Difference' in the neo-Victorian aesthetic is often presented as collision between nineteenth-century and modern history or culture. Graphic novels of this kind are packed with postmodern nods and winks: the ballad narrator in the *Century: 1910* volume of *The League of Extraordinary Gentlemen*, for example, whose Brechtian music-hall song undercuts the primary narrative from the perspective of the docklands' disenfranchised poor. These worlds are designed to defamiliarise: to create a thrill of recognition through the mask of strangeness. What happens when historical fact is turned on its head? How might the introduction of advanced technology alter the past, and our perception of it? How would the modern mind fare in this reimagined version of history? Neo-Victorianism also offers the chance to collapse the distinction between high and low culture, and imagine what happens when Jules Verne rubs up against exploitation movies, or when James Bond meets the Pre-Raphaelites.

When the everyday becomes odd, the opportunity arises to question our values, the assumptions we make, and the history we take for granted. Both Moore and Talbot are fascinated by how Britain got where it is today. This may relate to factual history (the Empire, the Industrial Revolution, military exploits), or to patriotism and national identity (how we see ourselves, and that which we define ourselves against). Both writers are interested in the underbelly of nationalist complacency – the dark deeds that have been done in the name of Queen and Country: what does 'Britishness' mean when the nation has had to rely on anarchist insurgents, or the torture of detainees, to earn its freedom?

The neo-Victorian graphic novel also excels at creating scenarios in which the politics of class, gender and race are retrospectively confronted via this prism of twisted logic. *The League of Extraordinary Gentlemen* rejects any cosy visions of past British glory. It presents a morally exhausted Britain, whose cynical establishment recruits a 'league' of outsiders: killers and monsters, led by a fallen woman, in which Nemo, the colonial interloper, is on hand to point out the hypocrisies inherent in the Empire's various crises. *Grandville* exhibits a similar revisionist tendency. In *Bête Noire*, the third instalment in Talbot's series, a street tableau is presented, in which the reader encounters a neo-Victorian version of Ford Madox Brown's iconic painting *Work* (1852–65) (Figs 6.2 & 6.3). Brown's picture was part of a nineteenth-century social realist drive to strip away pretention and ostentation, and reconnect art with everyday subject matter. In *Work*, the act of labour (intellectual or physical) possesses an inherent dignity and moral significance, beyond its simple economic value. In Talbot's reimagining, the road-digging navvies of Brown's version are replaced by blank-faced automatons and the working classes by 'doughfaces' (the human-like sub-class who share *Grandville*'s animal world). This is a reconfiguration of one of the key set-pieces of Victorian art, filtered through a steampunk fantasy, and serves simultaneously to reconnect neo-Victorianism

(FIG. 6.2)
BRYAN TALBOT, *GRANDVILLE
BÊTE NOIRE: A FANTASY*
(LONDON: JONATHAN CAPE,
2012), P. 30. IMAGE COURTESY
OF THE ARTIST.

(FIG. 6.3)
FORD MADOX BROWN,
WORK (1852–65). OIL ON
CANVAS. MANCHESTER ART
GALLERY.

6.2

with the politics and aesthetics of the nineteenth century, and to take it into the future – questioning the role and value of human 'work' in a world of machines.

A similar question is posed in *From Hell* – Moore and Campbell's dense and allusive reworking of the Whitechapel murders. Confronted with a prophetic vision of the late-twentieth-century digital revolution, William Gull (Jack the Ripper) cries out: 'Where comes this dullness in your eyes? How has your century numbed you so? Shall man be given marvels only when he is beyond all wonder?' Like Gull, the historical graphic novel looks backwards and forwards

6.3

at the same time, and the genre mirrors his claim to 'flicker in and out of history'. The Victorians are an ideal vehicle for these dystopian pasts and primitivist futures. They are all around us – chillingly demonstrated by Gull's occult circumnavigation of London, taking in streets, churches and other landmarks that still resonate with the city's residents. We live with the Victorians' ghosts, and the fruits of their labour – for good or evil – are our reward. Gull looks up from his bloody work to embrace the glass and steel metropolis of modern London (Fig. 6.4), and he speaks for the entire neo-Victorian project when he declares: 'For better or worse, the twentieth century. I have delivered it.'

(FIG. 6.4)
ALAN MOORE AND EDDIE
CAMPBELL, *FROM HELL*
(LONDON: KNOCKABOUT
COMICS, 2000), CH. 8, P. 40.
IMAGE COURTESY OF
KNOCKABOUT COMICS.

From Hell - Chapter 8 - Page 40.

6.4

—IS FOR—
THE RESTLESS PURSUIT OF ARTISTIC EXCELLENCE
AND TO HELL WITH THE CONSEQUENCES

WIRELESS
TIME TRAVEL

PAUL ST GEORGE

DEVELOPMENT OF WIRELESS TELEGRAPHY. SCENE IN HYDE PARK.
[These two figures are not communicating with one another. The lady is
receiving an amatory message, and the gentleman some racing results.]

7.1

There are many kinds of time travel.

(FIG. 7.1)
DEVELOPMENT OF WIRELESS
TELEGRAPHY. SCENE IN HYDE
PARK, PUNCH MAGAZINE (26
DECEMBER 1906), P. 451.

In this cartoon from 1907 (Fig. 7.1), 'the two figures are not
communicating with one another. The lady is receiving an amatory
message, and the gentleman some racing results'.

This is a kind of time travel of ideas. The author of the cartoon, Lewis
Baumer, *looks to the future from the past* and makes some predictions
about the social and cultural implications of a technological
innovation.

It is tempting to read this cartoon as a piece of contemporary
prochronism. But time travel is more complicated than the simplistic
dictionary definitions of parachronism, prochronism, retro-futurism
and so on would have us believe. We are left with an unsatisfying,
nagging doubt.

I am reminded of one glorious scene in Strauss's *Der Rosenkavalier*.
A lecherous older man is seducing a young woman. Unknown to
him, the young woman is actually a young man. But the audience
knows that this young man is actually portrayed by a woman.

(FIG. 7.2)
GEORGE DU MAURIER,
EDISON'S TELEPHONOSCOPE
(TRANSMITS LIGHT AS
WELL AS SOUND), PUNCH'S
ALMANACK FOR 1879,
[UNPAGINATED].

In a good story, different desires and layers of meaning can play against each other. Similarly, when we read this cartoon, it is not enough to say this is *the future as seen from the past*, we are looking at the past looking at the future from the future. And we do so with an inescapable suspicion that the whole thing might have been fabricated by some up-and-coming artist in an exhibition about Victorian revivalism.

Under this earlier cartoon from 1879 (Fig. 7.2) we read that:

(Every evening, before going to bed, Pater- and Materfamilias set up an electric camera-obscura over their bedroom mantel-piece, and gladden their eyes with the sight of their Children at the Antipodes, and converse gaily with them through the wire.)

Paterfamilias (*in Wilton Place*)	'Beatrice, come closer. I want to whisper.'
Beatrice (*from Ceylon*)	'Yes, Papa dear.'
Paterfamilias	'Who is that charming young Lady playing on Charlie's side?'
Beatrice	She's just come over from England, Papa. I'll introduce you to her as soon as the Game's over!'

The second example is not just a guess about the future from the past. The author, George du Maurier, shares in a public desire to shape the future he depicts. The imagined uses of a technology are being considered and described many years before the technology was available. But an underlying assumption is that the technology will be available, one day.

The future is described in terms that are borrowed from the past: camera obscura, electric, wire. This is time travel, but perhaps this is not fantasy or frivolous science fiction. Is it more accurate to say that du Maurier is taking part in research and development towards the invention of a new device?

And George du Maurier, the author of the 1879 cartoon, was not alone.

In 1877, the French editor Louis Figuier used the term 'Telectroscope' to popularise an invention he wrongly interpreted as real, and he ascribed this invented invention to Alexander Graham Bell. The word Telectroscope was typed in error, a simple typographical mistake. Figuier intended to write the words 'the electroscope'. Actually, the 'Telectroscope' described in the article had nothing to do with a real electroscope, and it had never existed.

Nevertheless the word 'Telectroscope' was widely accepted. It was used to describe the (false) claims of nineteenth-century inventors and scientists such as Constantin Senlecq, George R. Carey, Adriano de Paiva, and later Jan Szczepanik, whose experiments fascinated Mark Twain.

In 1898, Twain wrote a short story set in the near future. He called the story 'From the "London Times" of 1904' and in it he describes an invention called the 'Telelectroscope', a gadget hooked up to the phone system: 'The improved "limitless-distance" telephone was presently introduced, and the daily doings of the globe made visible to everybody, and audibly discussable too, by witnesses separated by any number of leagues.'

The aims and purpose of the Telephonoscope, Telelectroscope and the Telectroscope are remarkably similar.

Figuier's Telectroscope of 1877, du Maurier's Telephonoscope of 1879, and Mark Twain's Telelectroscope of 1898, all fictional, had a huge effect on the public and increased the demand for a 'device for the suppression of absence'.

To be clear, George du Maurier called his device Edison's Telephonoscope, but this was an invention. Edison had not invented the Telephonoscope, nor did he.

The inaccurate reports, the accidental hoax, the wishful thinking, the science fiction fantasies and popular imagination predicted and anticipated a machine that would serve the mission of '*la suppression de l'absence*' by facilitating real-time, face-to-face communication over vast distances.

Many inventors in many countries filed patents for an invention that would enable two-way live communication. Many years later, the word had changed (Telectroscope to Television), and the aims had been reduced to one-way broadcast but television was invented. The word 'Telectroscope' was eventually replaced by the term 'Television' in 1900.

But the Telectroscope (and so television) was invented by Figuier, du Maurier and Twain.

This public desire could exist and grow because then (and now I am *looking at the past from the future*), it seems as if desire came first and the technology was invented, developed and brought to market in response to that public desire.

It is my impression and understanding that there was something very different about the development of technology in the Victorian era. It seems that, then, people dreamt of, imagined, talked about, and wrote about new devices long before they were invented. Then (immediately or soon afterward), inventors would try to satisfy that public desire. Think of cinema, the bicycle, some aspects of photography, the telephone and television.

Nowadays, again it is my impression and understanding, there are fewer inventions and the sequence of events (1. market demand; 2. supply of technology) is reversed.

Nowadays it seems that we do not have inventions, we have incremental adaptations. It also seems that these adaptations are not in response to a market demand. Rather it seems that we are sold these adaptations and persuaded that we want them. So, now we have a technological adaptation of something already existing and advertising agencies and marketing companies spend a large proportion of the sales price to persuade us that we want this new (old) technology.

This persuasion usually includes making us feel insecure and disappointed about what we have and where we are.

Perhaps this is why I have joined a growing band of people who invoke 'Victorianness'. Perhaps our intention is to evoke that earlier, more hopeful and optimistic, attitude and to call out, in our humble ways, for technologists to return to giving us what we want and need rather than trying to persuade us that we want another adaptation of what we already have.

Our nostalgia is to be in some other time, that is not our own, when we could hope that some clever person was trying to make something that would meet our real needs – a time when we still believed in improvement, that things would get better: a Victorian time.

There must have been a certain magic at the time of the inception of a new invention. In my own Telectroscope (London and New York, 2008) I tried to deliver the promise of the first imaginings, the two-way, real-time, face-to-face communication over vast distances rather than the watered down, one-way broadcast of recorded programmes. I also tried to provide the viewer with the experience of what it might have been like to be there at the birth of a new technology, even though this particular technology never actually quite got there. We cannot appreciate the experience of the magic at the beginning of a cultural device's story by looking at a presentation or representation of the first device (even if it had existed). We would see this artefact through the filters of the intervening history, accompanied by our greater awareness and familiarity with the device and its descendants.

To recreate the magic, I use defamiliarisation or ostranenie (остранение).

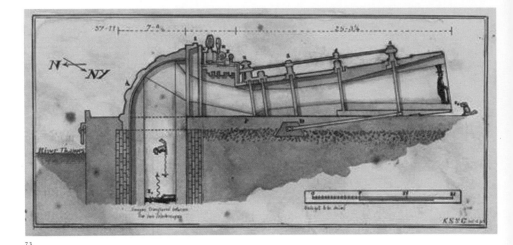

7.3

(FIG. 7.3)
PAUL ST GEORGE, *DESIGN
FOR THE TELECTROSCOPE*
(2008). ILLUSTRATION
BY FELIX BENNETT.
COPYRIGHT THE ARTIST.

Defamiliarisation is another kind of time travel. The Telectroscope takes its public audience back to the cusp of invention (Fig. 7.3). The magic of most inventions is overlooked as much of what we do is familiar. We take photographs, watch films, send messages, get from place to place at speeds that should make us faint, and most of the time, we think nothing of it.

Defamiliarisation can take us back to the cusp of time when the invention was new and unfamiliar, and so awaken us to the magic of much of what we can do with technology.

We all, I hope, encounter other people every day. But we do not jump up and down or behave like puppies in the park when we see other people. This, however, is what people do when they see other people through a Telectroscope. What is it about the Telectroscope that makes people behave in such a joyous and uninhibited way? The Telectroscope frames our view of other people so that the familiar, the overlooked, becomes unfamiliar again. Through the Telectroscope we see other people as if for the first time.

This is an aesthetic affect. Very simply, if anaesthetics send us to sleep, then an aesthetic work awakens us to an experience or an event. We can use this quick definition to understand Warhol's Brillo boxes. When Brillo boxes are displayed on the supermarket shelf we merely recognise them, or we do not see them at all. The most we are likely to do (pre-Warhol) is check them against our shopping list and decide whether we need to buy any or leave the oven dirty for another week. When Warhol took the Brillo boxes and placed them in a gallery window the boxes changed. Visitors to that gallery would not have merely recognised the boxes, they would have seen the boxes as if for the first time. The viewers confronted by the Brillo boxes in the art gallery would have been awakened, through defamiliarisation, to the humble cleaning pads. This example is useful as it also shows that the defamiliarisation effect wears off: it has a shelf life. Putting Brillo boxes in a window nowadays would have little or no aesthetic effect. We know too much about Brillo boxes and Warhol: they are now too familiar.

Just before the birth of an invention, the imminent technology belongs to a number of domains: the insane, the liar, the occult and science (Fig. 7.4).

For God's sake, go down to reception and get rid of a lunatic who's down there. He says he's got a machine for seeing by wireless! Watch him – he may have a razor on him.[1]

Some are insane to believe the invention process will be successful – seeing pictures at a distance, flight, seeing by wireless (pah!); some believe the impossible, but their faith is founded on the irrational, the esoteric, the occult; some file false patents in the hope of duping investors; and others base their hope on sounder scientific and engineering principles.

(FIG. 7.4)
PAUL ST GEORGE, *SQUARE OF OPPOSITIONS SHOWING RELATIONSHIPS BETWEEN SCIENCE, DECEPTION, THE OCCULT AND INSANITY.*

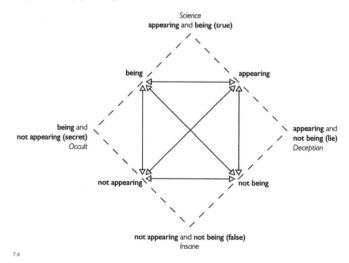

7.4

At the cusp, at the advent of a new invention, its audiences are confronted by the ambiguity of seeing (perhaps for the first time) what was recently impossible, unexplained, unbelievable or unknown. Before the invention exists each domain has a claim on its future. Once it has happened (at the beginning) the nascent invention will bring with it associations and traces from each of the antecedent discourses.

We can recapture part of this early strangeness through some of the short stories of H. G. Wells. Consider cinema and its early development in the last five years of Victoria's reign. To truly understand what it must have been like to encounter cinema for the first time we have to imagine it in an unfamiliar setting: to make it strange. A near perfect example is 'The Remarkable Case of Davidson's Eyes'. I will not provide a synopsis of the story. I am sure you have read it, or you will now. I want to tell instead the story of its writing. Wells, being a friend of the Lumière brothers, was one of the very first people ever to see cinema (a recording of an event projected on to a screen). 'Davidson's Eyes' was published in 1895, the year the Lumières held their first private screening of projected motion pictures.

In the story of Davidson and his eyes, an accident in a chemistry lab is a literary excuse for Wells to write about what it is like when one of your senses is divorced from the other four or five senses. This is not an imaginative short story; it is an account of audience response. Wells was the audience and his account describes his amazement at seeing a recording of an event in which sight is present in the recording but all the other senses are absent. This, then, was unfamiliar and so Wells was awakened to the experience and found cinema amazing – so much so that he wrote a story that attempts to convey that amazement to readers.

I try to imagine what it must have been like to see the first television picture, see the first film, or read the first telegram. I then try, following the example of Wells, to create an analogous experience that will give a contemporary audience that same thrill and joy.

The Televisor itself and Baird's plans for it would be pure science fact. About forty-eight years after it was first imagined by the *Punch* cartoonist du Maurier and others, the science that Baird dreamt of creating, a machine capable of letting you see people who are *in another place* – seeing by wireless – was still also science fiction, was still also insane.

For the exhibition at the Guildhall Art Gallery, I have delved into that very Victorian blurring of the boundaries between the presentation of science, spectacle and the occult. I have created a prototype Telectroscope modelled on Geißler tubes and Crookes tubes, devices that anticipated the Cathode ray tube (Fig. 7.5). In this, a viewer will see another viewer from another part of the Gallery. The experience will be similar to that enjoyed by Logie Baird when he first looked into his Televisor and saw Oliver Hutchinson from 'the other side'.

(FIG. 7.5)
ILLUSTRATION OF
GEIßLER TUBES AND
CROOKES TUBES, TAKEN
FROM MEISER & MERTIG,
PREISVERZEICHNIS NO. 27,
PHYSIKALISCHER APPARATE
UND CHEMISCHER GERÄTE
(CATALOGUE OF PHYSICAL
AND CHEMICAL APPARATUS
AND DEVICES) (LEIPZIG,
1903).

Geißler tube, Televisor, Crookes tube…

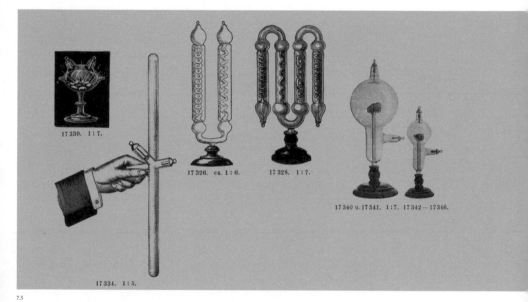

7.5

I am not trying to produce a facsimile demonstration. Indeed there is very little similarity between the apparatus Baird used and the device I have made. But I do hope that the experience of looking into the prototype Telectroscope and seeing another person will be as magical as that first television show.

And so the time travel continues…

---

1 Assistant editor at the *Daily Express* office on Fleet Street, on hearing that John Logie Baird was in the building.

NEO-VICTORIAN
TATTOOING

MATT LODDER

It is a simple truth that tattooing largely reflects the visual culture from which it emerges, at least in the West. In the sixteenth and seventeenth centuries, European pilgrims to the Holy Lands were tattooed with the devotional iconographies of their faith (crosses, Christograms, images of Christ). At the turn of the nineteenth century, tradesmen marked their skins with signs of their professions and sailors repeated on their bodies the suns, anchors and pierced hearts they carved into tobacco tins and whalebone whilst at sea. In the 1930s, Mickey Mouse appeared on the sheets of pre-drawn designs ('flash') which tattooists traded amongst themselves and advertised to customers.

The 1880s and 90s were the first heyday of professional tattooing in Britain, with the several high-end tattoo studios in the heart of London advertising their trade in socially aspirational publications such as *Country Life, Tatler* and the *Sporting Times*. In the moneyed salons of Victorian Britain, awash with Japanese imagery and artefacts since the Meiji Restoration of 1868, those of means and taste who were getting tattooed chose dragons, and snakes, and Orientalist demons, or, on occasion, laid out small fortunes and bore often dozens of hours of pain to have large reproductions of etchings by Reynolds, Constable and others permanently applied to their skin. Until the invention of the electric tattoo machine in the early years of the twentieth century, large-scale artistic tattooing was largely confined to those who could afford to spend the time and the money it would take to have their arms and backs covered in tattoos applied with slow, painstaking hand-tools, and so tattooists boasted (often not entirely truthfully) in articles in the popular press and amongst themselves of their upper-class clientele of aristocrats, princesses and kings (Edward VII was certainly tattooed in Jerusalem in 1862 and several British tattooers claimed to have tattooed him back at home, though no reputable primary source confirms this later coverage). Wealthy travellers ensured they were able to get 'authentic', complex tattoos in Japan, and the most wealthy of them even paid for their Japanese tattoo artists to travel back to Britain or America so that their friends could be tattooed by a real Japanese master.

In the early years of the twenty-first century, tattoo magazines on both sides of the Atlantic began to feature a new trend in contemporary tattooing. Suddenly, it seemed every tattooist in the anglophone world was being asked to tattoo images of men with moustaches and top-hats and monocles; pipes; women in corsets;

animals wearing ostentatious military garb; Singer sewing machines; penny farthings; pocket watches – in short, with images steeped with heavy-handed reference to the visual and material culture of the long nineteenth century and its recent reimaginings. The revival of Victorian aesthetics in other media since the middle of the twentieth century seems often to reproduce (or at least directly reference) those actually common during Victoria's reign, even if the act of reproduction occurs through an ironic or parodic lens: steampunk clothing looks, at its roots, like Victorian clothing and costume; Gothic horror mash-ups of bookplate etchings, as in the work of Dan Hillier, do make direct aesthetic reference to nineteenth-century photocollage. In tattooing, however, this is not the case. As the popularity of Victorian iconographies grew, it is unsurprising that the trend would be reflected in tattoo habits, and yet it is striking that neo-Victorianism manifests itself in tattooing not as a revival of Victorian tattoo practices, but in a reflection of what might loosely be called a Victorian 'mood' in wider visual culture, drawing upon the ironised tropes of Victorian visual culture from printmaking, painting and clothing in the construction of a new vernacular fundamentally unlike the tattooing which was actually popular in the Victorian period (Figs 8.1a–8.1b).

8.1A   8.1B

One particular design – and the reaction to it – is indicative. Valerie Vargas, a tattoo artist based at Frith Street Tattoo in London, tattooed a solid full sleeve design on a girl in 2009 which became so popular that she eventually removed it from her website portfolio, so inundated was she with requests to reproduce it, or its elements, on other customers. The commissioned sleeve features a moustachioed man in a top-hat and cravat on the upper arm tightly embracing a Romany woman, shielding her against a pall of fog which envelopes them. On the lower arm, the fog clears to reveal a filigreed heart encircling an eye, as if from a Victorian embroidery pattern, and a Poe-esque raven set against a shining full moon, clutching a golden jewelled ruby pendant in its beak. The scene is punctuated throughout with dark red roses. Every element of this tattoo is composed with precise reference to Victorianism, and all its components combine as if as a collage to produce a distinctly Victorian affect, heavy with sideways, knowing allusions to class, taste, manners, ostentation and the occult which saturate neo-Victorian revivals more generally. What this scene does not feature, however, is any elements which would have actually been present even in the full sleeve commissions from the latter part of the nineteenth century.

One image from a 1903 article in an English illustrated magazine provides an indicative comparison. In a biographical report on the work of famous London society tattoo artist Tom Riley – who claimed to have tattooed, amongst others, the Duke of Saxe-Coburg, Prince Christian Victor and Prince George of Greece – a picture

8.2

appears captioned 'A German lady, well known in society' (Fig. 8.2). The photograph features a woman in an expensive-looking, low-cut ruffled dress, her arms crossed over her chest. Her arms – like Vargas's twenty-first-century customers' – are heavily tattooed, covered in a

collage of designs, but hers are distinctly Orientalist, or Japonesque in character: birds, dragons, spiders, butterflies, snakes and beetles cover her left and right biceps and forearms as if pinned to her by some demented naturalist; design motifs commonly seen on furniture, fire-screens and decorative panels imported into Europe from Japan by the boatload in the nineteenth century adorn her skin. The visual culture of her time, and place, and class, is borne on her body, indicative (at least for a while) of her cultured tastes, her appreciation of the authentic Oriental arts, and her appropriation of the habits and fashions of royal personages throughout Europe. The result is remarkable, beautiful and strange – for a modern audience to whom this story of upper-class tattooing in the Victorian period is largely forgotten, the thought, let alone the image, of a nineteenth-century woman with such ornate and visually arresting tattoo work is certainly shocking, as it testifies to a moment in both social and visual cultures which, unlike the painting, decorative arts and even architecture of the same period, has never been revived, revered or reappropriated.

Most strangely of all, this German lady wears a bag, hood or veil over her head for the photo, her face entirely obscured save for two small eye-holes, through which she squints towards the camera. By 1903, tattooing had already begun to fall from fashion amongst the upper classes. Tastes had shifted, perhaps driven by the easier and cheaper access to large-scale tattoos after the invention of the electric tattoo machine, perhaps simply by the whims of fashion, and though tattoo artists such as Riley proclaimed their upper-class client base in their advertisements and interviews right through to the First World War. At the time of Victoria's death, tattooing had already passed its peak as an upper-class fancy. It is possible that the lady was not, in fact, an aristocrat, and the hood was a clever marketing device by Mr Riley to convince the readers of the magazine that his human canvasses were more blue-blooded than they actually were, but the most plausible explanation is simply that this tattooed woman wished to keep her habits private: as criminological and anthropological theories of tattooing's inherent primitivism and connection with barbarism seeped into polite anglophone circles from the continent, where they had been gaining traction after the work of Cesare Lombroso and Alexandre Lacassagne, tattooed aristocrats and debutantes increasingly hid their tattoos away. Clothing fashions of the late nineteenth and early twentieth centuries, especially for women, did not often expose vast acres of flesh to public view in any case, but this lady's choice to wear a hood for her photograph seems to imply, even as she boldly exposes her arms to the camera, some sense of shame, or embarrassment about having her name and reputation linked to an increasingly marginalised practice, or at least the desire to keep her tattoos private. (In an infamous similar example, Edith, Marchioness of Londonderry, who had been tattooed in Japan around 1900, caused something of a sensation in 1938 when the shortening of hemlines in womenswear trends revealed a hitherto-unknown snake tattoo coiled around her entire lower left leg.)

A historical amnesia has thus overcome popular understandings of tattooing's history. As Victorian tattoo trends were suppressed in the popular imagination even shortly after the height of the practice's popularity, these histories are today little known. Moreover, the design choices of these Victorian tattoo aficionados do not immediately resonate *as* Victorian in the present day, such that they do not carry the same allusions of class, taste, whimsy and mystery which ironic neo-Victorian reproductions in other media do. It is unsurprising, then, that those enamoured enough of Victorianism today that they would tattoo its visual referents on their bodies choose the moustache, the pocket watch and the penny farthing (often even in the same design!) over Japonisme or, as one nineteenth-century Scotch baronet was reported to have chosen, a copy of Sir Edwin Henry Landseer's puppy portrait *Dignity and Impudence* of 1839. Nevertheless, several contemporary tattoo artists do take the visual culture of Victorian painting more seriously in their work, and it is indeed possible to create neo-Victorian tattoos which do not rely entirely on an iconographic shorthand of nineteenth-century culture to imbue their work with an air of appreciation for the visual culture of late-nineteenth-century Britain.

The work of German tattoo artist Juergen Eckel, for example, looks both on paper and on skin as if it could have been lifted from the walls of the Guildhall; his portraits of women are reminiscent of the Pre-Raphaelites in the same way as John William Waterhouse's were – echoes of the Brotherhood in mood, and gaze, and composition; soft, fleshy figures wrapped in sheaths of heavy, flowing cloth, clutching flowers; delicate, strange, angular faces heavy with melancholy and a profound, measured sense of certainty. Other art-historical influences are evident (that of art nouveau in particular) and customers will still request moustachioed men and pocket watches on occasion, but in his work there is little room for overt irony or the straightforward, tongue-in-cheek comedy. Instead, his tattoos look Victorian in a most sincere fashion, darker and richer than much other neo-Victorian work and with studied reference to actual nineteenth-century source material in its production, from paintings to period-correct jewellery and design elements. The Gothic horror which saturates several of his pieces is profoundly Victorian in tone – ashen ravens often feature. Most importantly, however, Eckel is not studying the contours of Victorian visual culture in order to reproduce it directly; his work is not a parody of Victorian aesthetics, but a sure-footed set of responses to a visual culture he finds inspiring and beautiful more in tone than in motif.

In England, tattoo artist Rebecca Marsh – a collaborator and friend of Eckel's – treads a similar path, her tattoos, drawings and even workspace set firmly within nineteenth-century style without recourse to overt parodic reproduction (Figs 8.3a–8.3d). Marsh's interests lie in taxidermy – her tattoo shop is a veritable menagerie of long-dead animals, in the style of a Victorian cabinet of curiosities – and her tattoo work reflects this, with animals featuring prominently: her renderings of birds, foxes and cats resemble the taxidermied tableaux popular in the Victorian era, dressed in ornate jewels and framed on the skin in complexly drawn surrounds referenced from furniture, embroidery and costume. Marsh's work is lighter in tone than Eckel's, but she also avoids the ironic and the comic, each piece imbued with an honest, genuine and obvious love for the subject matter.

Though there has not, as yet, been a full-scale revival of Victorian tattooing, the influence of the nineteenth century in certain twenty-first-century tattoo habits is undeniable. The most successful neo-Victorian tattooing, it seems, is that which does not draw directly on twentieth- and twenty-first-century revivalist tropes, but which takes its aesthetic cues directly from the nineteenth century – even if those cues come overwhelmingly from media other than tattooing. Whilst there has been no shortage of jokey, hollow, irreverent neo-Victorian tattoos in recent years – having an ironic handlebar moustache tattooed on the inside of your index finger, such that it was possible to hold it above your top lip, actually briefly reached the status of a bona-fide 'trend' in 2003 – the work of tattoo artists whose connection to the Victorian period is in the moods of late-nineteenth-century art and design, rather than in its most easily recognised (and parodied) symbols show that much more interesting uses and re-uses of this most influential of periods in art history can be made on skin.

I
—IS FOR—
INCURABLE
ROMANTIC

RIP
DEAD
FROM
A
BROKEN
HEART

LACE

TOM GALLANT

Introduction

LACERE –
TO ENTICE;
TO ENSNARE

LAQUEUS –
TO DECORATE;
TO CONSTRICT

The relation between what we see and what we know is never settled.[1]

From a background in graphic design and printmaking, my research led me to an analysis of the language of folktales and the effect of the Industrial Revolutions on literature, societies and communities. A contemporary feminist viewpoint has inspired me to follow certain parallels drawn through the symbolism of the oppressed in visual culture and the hierarchies evident in the histories of crafts and decorative arts. The nature of telling, as a conceptual framework, has enabled me to make connections between a visual vocabulary and a historical platform. At the core of my practice lies the abusive or absent male in our society and the force of industry that overwhelms all that is female in our culture: a simultaneous liberation and exploitation through work (Fig. 9.1).[2]

My first collection took John Fowles' novel *The Collector* (1963) as a metaphor for the male oppressor at every level in society. With Miranda as his ill-fated but well-matched heroine Fowles' work is a multi-layered discourse on ideas connecting science, the arts, British colonialism and, of course, the British class structure then and today. I used the Natural History Museum's online archive for its collection of Eastern Palaearctic moths and cut their silhouettes onto interior details from magazines of Asian girls photographed for Western magazines. Pinned to a wall in a grid of 108, the lighting projects their shadows. Left open to the movement of air, they flutter freely, frequently being coerced by breath (Fig. 9.2).[3]

For my second collection, Charlotte Perkins Gilman's 1892 novella 'The Yellow Wallpaper' provided a more profound framework for influences that relate to my current practice (Fig. 9.3). Its author conveys a claustrophobic world inhabited by a Victorian wife passively imprisoned by her husband. In decaying plants and fine lace, smoke and rain, the cobwebs coating the banqueting hall in *Great Expectations*, and the pine trees outside Thérèse Desqueyroux's rain-spattered windows, the imprisonment of women in the institution of marriage reveals itself.

Subsequently I have explored languages of pattern that reflect a desire to control. I am fascinated by beauty as subterfuge for the

9.1

9.2

9.3

erotic and the obscene, using familiar devices and motifs. In my work the aesthetics of nature seen through the eyes of craft and design create a deceptive layer that seduces the viewer before revealing its content. This essay is no exception. I hope to convey my practice in the context of lace without having to describe it overtly or map its history. I am fascinated by motifs that carry interwoven layers of meaning, and the obviousness of lace[4] as a message bearer has prevented me from using it, whilst recognising it as an important simile.[5]

Nonetheless, lace appears in my work in indirect ways. In *Fuji Under Clouds* (2011) a page of text, from an early 1970s magazine, with a pornographic colour image on the reverse is cut to the shape of the words (Fig. 9.4). This paper cut is sandwiched between glass and floated one centimetre above a white mount. The page originated from a time when including educational articles in stag mags enabled publishers to bypass censorship laws. Through the removal of the text it is possible to see the colour reflected off the mount and, through the net, to spy revealing flesh tones and form. Thus the work acts as the membrane through which our gaze passes and is also the subject of our gaze.

(FIG. 9.1)
TOM GALLANT, WITH MARIOS SCHWAB, *DRESS 09* (2008). LASER-CUT CORDED SILK, PRINTED SILK CRÊPE. CRAFTS COUNCIL COLLECTION. COPYRIGHT THE ARTISTS. PHOTOGRAPH BY ALEX LEE.

(FIG. 9.2)
108 MOTHS (2004). CUT PAPER, GLASS. COPYRIGHT THE ARTIST.

(FIG. 9.3)
DETAIL OF *IRIS* (2012). DIGITALLY PRINTED VINYL WALLPAPER. COPYRIGHT THE ARTIST. PHOTOGRAPH BY SOPHIE MUTEVELIAN.

(FIG. 9.4)
FUJI UNDER CLOUDS (2010). CUT PAPER, GLASS. COPYRIGHT THE ARTIST.

9.4

A desire to return to the handmade led me to the earliest craft using paper.[6] After receiving a gift of Chinese paper cuts I had a eureka moment. I was instantly drawn to the paper cuts' ability to transcend cultural differences and material stereotypes and, most importantly, they were clearly both print and sculpture. The first works I made were copies of these designs onto pornographic magazines and it was immediately apparent that the cut had transferred a preciousness, fragility and value onto the disposable. Furthermore, the depth obtained by the pressure of cutting by hand into a rubber mat, the knife splaying the edges and catching the light, gave a more profound visual relationship than industrial techniques. From the bride's veil to the hand-cut fretwork of a Catholic confessional, the labour involved in creating these membranes bears value, greater than its function. The individual adds to the abstract language of this barrier with a charge linked to the unveiling and in doing so imbues the object with greater fetishistic power, even beauty.

In 2006 I made *British Birds*, a collection that uses amateur photographs as source material. The series is an examination of the amateur photographer and scientist that connects the leisure pursuits of the upper classes of the Victorian age to the contemporary working class. Cut directly from readers' wives magazines, works were collaged in several layers between glass to give the illusion of form and colour, and the look of traditional taxidermist collections as well as botanical illustrations. I also wanted to play with innuendo and the associations with the names of the birds and twitchers (Fig. 9.5).[7]

(FIG. 9.5)
FIRECREST (2006). CUT PAPER, GLASS. COPYRIGHT THE ARTIST. PHOTOGRAPH BY ANDY KEATS.

9.5

Paper cutting has a long and varied history in the hands of the storyteller and the Eastern European folk artist and under the knives of many contemporary artists.[8] No example is more inspirational than the animations of Lotte Reiniger, who made the first feature-length animation film – *The Adventures of Prince Achmed* (1926) – using cut silhouettes. There is an ethereal beauty in the depth of shadow and the play with light and form that transfixes. These films have their origin in Chinese shadow puppet theatre as much as the shadows in Plato's Cave. This relationship to our own shadow only increases the fascination with the silhouette – from the European mythology of the undead without shadow or reflection, to the eugenics of phrenology and the belief that the profile of man reveals his status, tendency to crime and the superiority of certain races over others.

The Industry of Motifs

You may be sure that any decoration is futile, and has fallen into at least the first stage of degradation, when it does not remind you of something beyond itself, of something of which it is but a visible symbol.[9]

In *Chrysanthemum* (2005), a wallpaper design by William Morris is dissected into a repeat and then two layers; these are cut from the pages of hardcore pornographic magazines (Fig. 9.6). The repeat is cut six times and each layer collaged between glass. The graphic detail becomes abstracted through the overlapping cuts. The repeat draws out colour, details and forms that flow and join each layer. The brain

9.6

(FIG. 9.6)
CHRYSANTHEMUM (2005).
CUT PAPER, GLASS.
COPYRIGHT THE ARTIST.
PHOTOGRAPH BY ANDY
KEATS.

fights to see and unsee, as the veil is simultaneously erotic and graphic. The stems, leaves and petals distort the image and the two layers complement and obstruct. The shapes join with the pattern and the pattern distorts to follow the contorted bodies.

The following series, *The Collector III*, was devised as six framed works positioned around a floor piece based on the Ardebil Carpet in the V&A. Examining the currency of domestic interiors behind amateur photographs of readers' wives and the folly of topiary, they aim to convey the moment in 'The Yellow Wallpaper' when the main protagonist becomes one with the wallpaper – nature turned graphic.[10] *Iris* (2005) follows a repeat pattern using copies of the same hardcore magazine, with two layers of artwork separated and sandwiched by glass and additional layers of floral and bird elements on top. The form has been literally and figuratively cut away while allowing the pattern to grow organically (Fig. 9.7).

Ever since our ancestors were hunting and being hunted, our brain has been stimulated by the illusory challenge of understanding pattern and the hidden image. The brain is constantly hiding and revealing, seeing and unseeing the new and the familiar. It finds patterns and coincidences where there are none and revels in the rewards of remembering faces and reading complex figurative forms reduced to a graphic logo. From handprints in caves, to bulls' horns on the palace at Knossos and Doge Leonardo Loredan's cloak, my fascination is part of a continuing narrative enhancing and reducing the world around us. It is born out of the folk traditions that were driven into industry through colonial power struggles for dominance over local crafts and skills, cultivating global trade routes and with them slave cultures. The main motifs in my work originate from museum cultures and religious iconography, and are connected to the effect that various industries have had on communities.[11] These are designs that represent both liberal and exploitative views in a visual culture that spans the breadth of art history.

However, the particular era that underpins the visual language in my work is the Victorian: a culture perpetually in the light of its own success, having to shade its eyes from the speed of its transformation (Fig. 9.8). This society, which pervades every corner of our present, describes the turning of an innocent. The brutal childishness of the nineteenth century is at once seductive and repellent. From the accounts of Friedrich Engels' experience of the mills and mines to

the purity of the fascination with photography, each step forward was made on the backs of the demoralised and enslaved masses.[12] I feel that it is this overwhelming purity of capitalist greed that leaves such a bitter-sweet aftertaste and so rich an artistic seam to tap. The simple hierarchies of the class system, an Empire never in the dark and the moral code that shored up its backbone for a rapidly expanding society demoralised to the degree of being described as animalistic. From lace cloth supposedly covering sexualised piano legs to studio portraits of dead children, the Victorian has the drama of horror and perversity, the shock of the new and the undead past clinging to the ankle-length skirts of its matrons.

La Petite Mort

Today, nobody recognises that eroticism is an insane world whose depths, far beyond its ethereal forms, are infernal.[13]

Would I to Those (2009), is an appropriation of Gustave Doré's illustration of Paulo and Francesca, itself a reappropriation of Ary Scheffer's paintings (Fig. 9.9). All of the surrounding image is removed, leaving a ghost of cloth and its intertwined lovers. It is part of a series, *The Collector V*, that relates to the erotically charged patterns and folds in Japanese ukiyo-e prints as well as the symbolism of cloth in religious iconography, painting and in particular wooden sacred altarpieces.[14] They are a move from a two-dimensional space into a three-dimensional vocabulary. Equally concealing and revealing, the middle layer of medieval patterns draws the gaze through the cut lines into the flesh behind – the repetitive nature of design mimicking the banality of the source material: pornographic magazines.

The moment when eroticism was born is strongly connected to religion, and both are linked to the language of death – whether the screen that separates the confessor and priest, or the idea of the church being a membrane between worshippers and the word of god, this vessel celebrates life and death in equal measures and with equal weight.[15] There is great sadness in a society where that which is held most sacred, from sex to death, the agony and the ecstasy, is deemed private. It is the act of separating ourselves from the animal that leaves us caged, anxious and fearful of our own nature. Above all it is a game of power and control, using social mores that govern our actions in public and drive our taboos into a private domain, oppressing instinct for the maintenance of hierarchies.

Like pornography, religion has constantly played its part in the development of transgressive cultures and the culture of transgression, from the early depictions of nudity and hell and the trials of witches, to the iconography of martyrs, and of course Christ. It is this interplay with seemingly disparate subjects that will continue to drive my research into historical mores and their effects on current trends, together with the desire to make public that which we hold private. As is the case with faith, the classification of the erotic is dependent on the individual's psyche and is wholly subjective. However, when both meet capitalism they become dictatorial and their only hope of existence is in taking the superior or ontological position against the consumer, defining rather than enabling choice.

My work is a veil between my private world and the public gaze, the space between confessor and priest, naked flesh and lover, between widow and mourner. This act of separation through removal, layering and pattern draws my practice into the medium and message. It appears to create a neutral platform that attracts confessions as much as questions, and encourages fruitful collaborations as it creates splendid isolation. The attention that various bodies of work have acquired is based largely on the technique as opposed to the conceptual framework and it has been for this reason that my focus has shifted towards changing the scale and mediums I work with. Whether in revealing the language behind the veil or readdressing the context in which the veil is seen, what continues to drive me is the desire to confess my inner thoughts and express them in a way that reveals more to the audience about themselves than my singular voice. Seeing through the lace curtain from the interior to the exterior.

2 From 'Arbeit Macht Frei', to the 'liberation from housewifery through work' of Nella Last (Housewife, 49).

3 The number 108 represents the number of Tibetan Buddhist sins, and the number of times a Japanese monk bangs a gong to purge sin for the previous year.

4 Lace is too often used as a popular motif for eroticism and grief in contemporary film, photography and literature (whilst acknowledging the importance of its profound link to exploitation through its colonial histories, early trade routes and of course a dissolution of local communities and traditions by industry).

5 It is worth noting to the reader, as I do to myself, that I found great difficulty in not mentioning lace throughout this essay and could have easily replaced it for any subject matter discussed. Hence, the decision to leave it to the reader to make the comparison.

6 Paper was invented in China in 834AD and the earliest craft of paper cutting began soon after. Initially used as window decorations these were later used in embroidery by the Japanese.

7 A birdwatcher whose main aim is to collect sightings of rare birds.

8 The act of cutting an illustration whist recounting a tale gave the illusion of the teller as medium, shaman between this world and the next, and for children between their world and that of the adult – the object of many of the tales' grievances.

9 William Morris, 'Some Hints on Pattern Designing' (1881), in *News From Nowhere and Other Writings* (London: Penguin, 1998), p. 260.

10 'I wonder if they all come out of that wallpaper as I did? But I am securely fastened now by my well-hidden rope – you don't get *me* out in the road there! I suppose I shall have to get back behind the pattern when it comes night, and that is hard! It is so pleasant to be out in this great room and creep around as I please!' Charlotte Perkins Gilman, 'The Yellow Wallpaper' (1892), in *The Yellow Wallpaper and Other Stories* (Mineola, NY: Dover, 1997), p. 14.

11 I use the word communities to represent the literal as well as a more contemporary reading of shared interest groups. The industries of printing and textiles both have their history of abuse, power struggles and effect on producers and consumers alike.

12 The irony of the abolition of slavery preceding the conditions in Lancashire mills and Welsh mines during the 1830s and 40s was not lost on the young Engels.

13 Georges Bataille, *The Tears of Eros* (1961), trans. Peter Connor (San Francisco: City Lights Books, 1989), p. 69.

14 It is perhaps interesting to note that I designed and worked on the series whilst developing designs for the first collection with Marios Schwab (Autumn/Winter 2008). *Dress 09* had a particular effect on my relationship to the imagery of cloth and use of pattern to change the focus of the viewer.

15 The word describes a container as well as a transient object (e.g. a ship), and is symbolic throughout mythology and religion, from the boat on the River Styx to Viking and Hindu funerals.

A —IS FOR— **ANTEPENULTIMATE**

SHADES OF MODERN GOTHIC, FROM THE VICTORIANS TO THE SURREALISTS

GILDA WILLIAMS

I.

In her essay 'Character in Fiction' (1924), Virginia Woolf wrote that 'on or about December 1910, human character changed', pinpointing a dramatic break with the shackles of the bygone Victorian era, happily replaced by the brave new world of Modernism. Among the pre-twentieth-century literary throwbacks that Woolf admonished was the terror genre, or 'Gothic': the sensationalist, eighteenth- and nineteenth-century popular favourite which combined Romance with horror, exotic and the supernatural. In uncompromising critical essays such as 'Gothic Romance' (1921), Woolf rejected the age-old terror fiction as an outmoded and unwanted, pre-Modern, pre-psychoanalytic literary tradition: a regression of an earlier age, to be erased from literary memory.

In both architecture and literature – despite vastly contrasting disciplinary remits – the descriptors 'Gothic', 'Gothic revival' or 'Victorian' often prompted in the early twentieth century unsympathetic associations with an outworn past which contrasted badly with Modernist experimentation and optimism. Even Kenneth Clark, author of *The Gothic Revival* (1928) and quasi-supporter of the Victorian-age architecture, spent much of his Introduction apologising for writing about a style of such candid distaste, which produced buildings Clark plainly dismisses as 'monsters' and 'unsightly wrecks'. 'The real reason that the Gothic Revival has been neglected is that it produced so little on which our eyes can rest without pain', wrote Clark unapologetically of the Victorians' chosen building style, ensuring that he was not mistaken for a cultural commentator out of touch with the Modernist/anti-revivalist sympathies of his day.[1]

On surprisingly consistent terms across disciplines, for committed Modernists like Woolf or Theodor Adorno (in literature), and later Clement Greenberg (in art), the departed nineteenth century and affiliated terms such as 'Gothic' or 'Victorian' represented all that was corrupt and inadmissible from the cultural past, to be replaced *tout court*. With regard to literature, in 'The Culture Industry Reconsidered' (1967) Adorno singled out the Gothic as the most pernicious sub-product that the culture industry has to offer, a deplorable commodity barely able to disguise its vulgar profit motive. In *After the Great Divide: Modernism, Mass Culture and Postmodernism* (1986), Andreas Huyssen sets Adorno's anti-mass cultural position for literature in parallel to Greenberg's condemnation of kitsch in art: 'the Other of modernism, the specter that haunts it, the threat against which high art has to shore up its terrain.'[2] As with Woolf and Adorno writing about literature, in nearly all of Greenberg's art writings his opposition between 'Modern' and 'Gothic' is straightforward: 'Modern' carries within it the promise of future, 'Gothic' signals an intolerable vestige of the past. For Greenberg, even his *protégé* Jackson Pollock possessed one damning limitation: a paralysing connection to the Gothic:

For all its Gothic quality, Pollock's art is still an attempt to cope with urban life; it dwells entirely in the lonely jungle of immediate sensation, impulses and notions, therefore is positivist, concrete. Yet its Gothic-ness, its paranoia and resentment narrow it.[3]

For Greenberg, terms like 'Gothic', 'Victorian' or the later 'Surrealist' were catastrophically out of step with the sweeping, masterful Modernism that he famously envisioned. The Gothic was haunted and suffocating whereas Modernism was free, carving giant walls of glass for light to pour inside and illuminate any lingering nineteenth-century shadows (a point vividly made in Anthony Vidler's *The Architectural Uncanny*, 1992). Greenberg abhorred 'Victorian mud and darkness' – a murkiness mercifully replaced by 'iridescence' by the turn of the century.[4] To paraphrase T. J. Clark, 'Gothic' – perhaps like its cousin 'Victorian' – was code for an 'art [that] could sink no lower', to be briskly swept aside in order to blaze the path of a shining Modernism.[5]

For many decades now, Greenberg's position as the leading spokesman for the period has been severely tested, with dissident histories – that of Surrealism, most notably – potently reappraised. In this spirit we might observe contradictory, contemporaneous positions to Greenberg's cultural and terminological prejudices. The following essay will examine early-twentieth-century practitioners who, by rejecting Greenbergian paradigms, refused such a demarcation and embraced notions of Gothic as progressive and liberating. Among these, the Bauhaus took inspiration from Victorian stalwart John Ruskin, who proposed medieval architecture as a model for an egalitarian future. And Surrealist spokesman André Breton considered Gothic literature – with its reliance on dreams and semi-rational states – not as a pre-Modernist anachronism (as it was for Woolf and Adorno) but as inspiration for emancipatory,

SHADES OF MODERN GOTHIC

subconscious creative strategies. This essay will firstly lay out the terms by which the paired terms 'Victorian' and 'Gothic' were cross-disciplinarily contrasted with their redeemer, 'Modernism'; thereafter, these oppositional assumptions will be complicated by some conflicting examples that welcomed Gothic as a symbol of the future. From the Victorian era into early Modernism, the historically imprecise term 'Gothic' served as a flexible placeholder able to represent contrasting moments across the cultural and political spectrum, from extreme left to right; progress to regress; communist triumph to capitalist might – all co-existing side by side. Shades of 'Gothic' were manipulated and readily put to work to fulfil opposing agendas and rewrite whatever symbolic histories were forcibly projected upon it.

II.

Conventionally, English-language Gothic fiction was launched in 1764 with the publication of the proto-novel *The Castle of Otranto* by Horace Walpole, the spoiled and propertied youngest son of long-time prime minister Sir Robert Walpole. The amateur architect/decorator of the noted Gothic revival architectural founding work Strawberry Hill (Twickenham, 1747–76), Walpole impulsively sub-titled *The Castle of Otranto* 'A Gothic Story', thus dragging together the medieval architectural style with a newly minted form of sensationalist literature – and ushering in centuries of terminological confusion thereafter, across two unrelated yet bizarrely overlapped disciplines: medieval buildings and popular horror. The craze for these early Gothic 'ghost stories' soared to mainstream heights around the turn of the nineteenth century with novelists such as Ann Radcliffe, Matthew Lewis, and (later) Mary Shelley, the genre's features crystallising into a set of recognisable staples: a cavernous ancient pile, family secrets, patriarchal brutes, female innocents, the undead and the supernatural. Even before the last wave of these early Gothic classics (Charles Maturin's *Melmoth the Wanderer*, 1820, and James Hogg's *Private Memoirs and Confessions of a Justified Sinner*, 1824) the genre began to feel stale, and had even set about ridiculing itself as with Jane Austen's parody, *Northanger Abbey* (1819).

Just as the Victorian era saw Gothic revival architecture evolve from Walpole's eighteenth-century, faux-aristocratic, hedonistic pleasure palace into the Victorians' exuberantly English civic structures

10.1

(perhaps best exemplified in the shining Palace of Westminster; 1840–70, by architect Charles Barry, with ornamentation by Pugin) (Fig. 10.1), so too the mid-to-late nineteenth century saw literary Gothic return to life with a new mission. The late-eighteenth-century's Gothic 'romances' – all swooning maidens and lecherous patriarchs – were retrieved as the ideal vehicle for a new generation of socially critical, psychologically rich, and sexually ambiguous fiction. These include *Jane Eyre* (Charlotte Brontë, 1847); *Carmilla* (Joseph Sheridan Le Fanu, 1872); *The Picture of Dorian Gray* (Oscar Wilde, 1890); and *Dracula* (Bram Stoker, 1899) – although these novels were rarely described then as 'Gothic', because the term was reserved at the time strictly for all things medieval. In these fictions, the early terror genre's distant landscapes of 'barbaric' Catholic faraway lands were replaced by dark passages closer to home: the newly 'satanic', industrialised landscape of England and, often, the unexplored recesses of London. The haunted hallways and secrets concealed within pointed-arch piles of late-eighteenth-century fiction were replaced by Victorian London's shadowy alleyways, and further symbolised by the toxic thoroughfares of the protagonist's own seething, insalubrious mind.

In architecture, the publication of *A History of the Gothic Revival* (Charles Eastlake, 1872) is said to mark the final years in which the Victorian pointed-arch revival was still considered a viable, nationalistically evocative style, connoting proud cultural values that nobly continued in, rather than unimaginatively cited, an ancient 'indigenous' style. By the early 1880s however, such an appraisal was rapidly losing ground, and the Gothic began to be described as outmoded and 'dead'. By the early twentieth century, staunch Modernists like the Italian Futurist leader Filippo Marinetti harshly dismissed John Ruskin's nostalgic veneration of Venetian medieval architecture, an attitude the Italian condemned as 'deplorable' and 'morbid', mired in a despicably 'passéist' picture of Italy.[6]

In the first decades of the twentieth century, for many arch-Modernists a predilection for the over-decorated Gothic was considered a mark of youthful and uncultivated tastes, prone to an excessive emotional reaction which Modernist-era rationalism was keen to stamp out. One of Georges Bataille's early texts, *Notre-Dame de Rheims* (1918), reminisces wistfully about the author's childhood spent in the shadow of the legendary cathedral, a Romanticist attitude Bataille stridently abandoned in later writings. So too the avant-garde musician John Cage claims to have harboured a budding interest in medieval architecture in his youth, a curiosity violently 'kicked out' of him by a well-meaning college professor who urged him to drop such antiquated interests forthwith, and turn his attention to a more worthwhile pursuit, Modernist architecture.[7]

Almost eighty years later, in an essay by the late-Conceptualist Andrea Fraser, 'Isn't this a wonderful place?' (2003), the artist acidly critiqued the audio-tour created for the opening of Frank Gehry's Guggenheim Bilbao, a self-congratulation which opens with a banal comparison between the shining new gallery spaces and a medieval church. 'Isn't this a wonderful place? It's uplifting. It's like a Gothic cathedral', the audio gushes, advancing a sense of the contemporary museum as a 'temple of art' whose enjoyment is immediately sensual, 'timeless', and secularly spiritual: presumably, for Fraser, an embarrassing and populist art cliché.[8] Across the twentieth century, 'Gothic' is often a stand-in descriptor for out-of-date, unsophisticated cultural products – whether in the immediate appeal of incense-filled, pointed-arch Christian minsters, or sensationalist and juvenile Gothic literature and horror film. Huyssen argues persuasively in *After the Great Divide* that popular and women's culture were regularly positioned within Modernist rhetoric as retrograde and antithetical to authentic culture, which in turn was the prerogative of men, establishing an ongoing contrast between high/male and low/female tastes. 'Victorian' (named after the matriarch–queen), like

'Gothic' (its fiction sometimes dubbed 'feminine fantasy fiction') were both in alliance with female and lowbrow culture, and hardly merited the serious attention of a masculine Modernism.

III.

In contrast with this disparaging early-twentieth-century opinion of Gothic, as regards architecture, the best known English art critic of the Victorian period John Ruskin was passionately enamoured with the art of the Middle Ages. Since at least the writings of Gothic scholar and fanatic A. W. G. Pugin in the 1830s, the age-old church architecture was packaged as an alluring combination of faith, aesthetics, and a morally responsible citizenry.[9] With the publication of Ruskin's essay 'The Nature of Gothic' (1851–53), a Christian spirit of community and the promise of socio-artistic progress were definitively pulled together around a symbolic revisitation of the Middle Ages. Tirelessly studying and drafting the minutiae of medieval architecture, Ruskin was eager to locate some essential moral source for the superiority of the Gothic style over the Classical, beyond mere stylistic difference. The English critic eventually arrived at the imaginative conclusion that the manufacture of a medieval cathedral implies within it a thriving community of co-operating artworkers – stone masons, glass cutters, carvers, weavers, and sculptors. Such a beneficent and productive social and artistic milieu, Ruskin lamented, was woefully absent in the alienating modern world:

[G]o forth again to gaze upon the old cathedral [...] for they are signs of the life and liberty of every workman who struck the stone; a freedom of thought, and rank in scale of being such as no laws, no charters, no charities can secure; but which it must be the first aim of all Europe at this day to regain for her children.[10]

In contrast to this picture-postcard fantasy of the Gothic cathedral's happy society of busy craftsmen, co-operating in their designated tasks like bees building the hive, Ruskin despised the perfect symmetry of the Classical building for the terrible signs not only of a slavishness to architectural principles, but of actual tyrannous architects yoked to equally tyrannous leaders, physically and creatively enslaving their beleaguered artisans. The pointed-arch cathedral for Ruskin becomes evidence of a functioning democracy comprised of art-loving and -making citizens, all enlisted in the creation of a magnificent, lasting artefact. In that socially minded spirit, Ruskin – and, subsequently, the younger William Morris – wished to recuperate an idealised, English, pre-Reformation artistic past.

With the Ruskinian conception of Gothic, the style becomes at once artistically liberating, socially progressive, and spiritually fulfilling – particularly for those blessed with an artistic temperament. Ruskin's labour-based conceptualisation of Gothic was later co-opted and reframed within a Germanic and Modernist visual paradigm in Lyonel Feininger's roughly executed woodcut *Cathedral of the Future* (Fig. 10.2). Feininger's shining symbol for the new Bauhaus, with its angular spires and primitive flying buttresses, glorified a stylised village church: a modest yet potently optimistic symbol of the future, repositioning Ruskinian/Victorian Gothic symbolism at the service of a Modernist socio-cultural agenda.

The Gothic's endless shape-shifting abilities allow it dramatically to switch symbolic political alliances: after the Victorian era's majestic and mighty English Gothic (its Parliament stretching to the length of almost three football pitches along the Thames), the style is put to work to symbolise the Bauhaus's Ruskinian-inspired association of the style with a small-scale, thriving artistic democracy.

In literature, despite Adorno or Woolf's condemning view of the old fiction, Gothic tales enjoyed status as a unique source of inspiration among the Surrealists. In André Breton's 'Limits Not Frontiers of Surrealism' (1936), the Surrealist spokesman claimed that dreams, memories, and other semi-rational emotional sources that Horace Walpole claimed as the inspiration for *The Castle of Otranto* should be reintroduced as valid tactics for Modernist-era creative work.[11] (In 1956 Theodor Adorno categorically refused Walpole's claims; 'no one dreams that way', he decried.)[12] The Surrealists represent an example of a significant twentieth-century artistic avant-garde movement which displayed a sustained interest in Victorian-era terror fiction, for example Emily Brontë's *Wuthering Heights* (1847). Bataille wrote in 1957 of 'the moral significance of the revolutionary nature of Emily Brontë's imagination and dreams' which he and others in the Surrealist circle – among them Antonin Artaud and Tristan Tzara – admired in that novel.[13] Though never fully a Surrealist, the artist Balthus compared his youth to that described in *Wuthering Heights*, and in 1935 created a series of lithographs

Lyonel Feininger   Cathedral

10.3

(FIG. 10.2 OPPOSITE)
LYONEL FEININGER,
KATHEDRALE (CATHEDRAL)
(1919). WOODCUT. MUSEUM
OF MODERN ART, NEW
YORK. GIFT OF ABBY
ALDRICH ROCKEFELLER.
COPYRIGHT THE ARTIST'S
ESTATE. IMAGE COURTESY
OF THE MUSEUM OF
MODERN ART, NEW YORK/
SCALA, FLORENCE.

(FIG. 10.3)
DOROTHEA TANNING,
*A MRS. RADCLIFFE
CALLED TODAY* (1944). OIL
ON CANVAS. PRIVATE
COLLECTION. COPYRIGHT
THE ESTATE OF DOROTHEA
TANNING, ADAGP, PARIS
AND DACS, LONDON.

published in *Minotaure* of Emily Brontë's supernatural tale, depicting the protagonist Catherine as a sexually provocative young girl cast into dangerous scenarios to which she responds with charged defiance. Like Balthus, virtually all the artists of repute who have taken terror literature as their subject matter can be seen as falling well outside of the Greenbergian abstracting tunnel-vision, following instead a figurative and illustrational model plainly at odds with the trajectory of Modernist abstraction. Among these we find the quasi-Surrealist Dorothea Tanning, who brought literary and architectural strains of 'Gothic' together in paintings such as *A Mrs. Radcliffe Called Today* (Fig. 10.3).

For the Surrealists and their followers, art inspired by terror literature claimed an affinity with the earlier fiction by virtue of shared methodology (dreams) as well as content (the irrational and the mysterious; erotically ambiguous scenarios), all represented through an illustrational pictorial language aimed at an enigmatic form of visual storytelling. The Surrealists' multiple evocations of Gothic are among the reasons Greenberg abhorred the movement; for Greenberg, Surrealism was Gothic, and this represented all that Modernism wisely rejected:

The Surrealists, promoting a newer renascence of the Spirit *of* Wonder, *have cast back to those periods after the Middle Ages which were fondest of the marvellous and which most exuberantly exercised the imagination: the Baroque, the late eighteenth century, and the Romantic and Victorian nineteenth century. Surrealism has revived all the Gothic revivals and acquires more and more of a period flavour, going in for Faustian lore, old-fashioned and flamboyant interiors, alchemistic mythology and whatever else are held to be excesses in taste of the past.*[14]

Greenberg catalogues here a cross-historical density of negative associations with 'Gothic' and 'Victorian', gathering within them all that in art is retrograde, decorative and nostalgic – in sum, all that marks the 'bad' (non-Modernist) art and the weakest art-historical moments of the past ('the Baroque, the late eighteenth century and the Romantic and Victorian nineteenth century'), across lesser disciplines ('Faustian lore, old-fashioned and flamboyant interiors, alchemistic mythology'). 'Victorian' or 'Gothic' served as a shorthand for all that is excessive and stifling about pre-Modernist art.

Even prominent post-Greenbergian reassessments of Surrealism undertaken by American scholars such as Rosalind Krauss and Hal Foster all but omit the Gothic sources from their research; the Gothic appears only in a pair of footnotes in Foster's *Compulsive Beauty* (1993).[15] It seems as if, even in recuperating for late twentieth-century audiences the Surrealist art that Greenberg had ignored, a later generation of post-Modernist art historians felt it equally necessary to ignore its unpalatable connections with literary Gothic, part of the dated, irrecuperable, Bretonian side of Surrealism. In *Compulsive Beauty*, Foster drew together the many strands of Surrealism within the rubric of the 'the uncanny', the subject of one of Freud's final great texts. In some ways Sigmund Freud represents the emblematic figure able to draw together the disparate strands uniting Modernism, Gothic, Surrealism, and nineteenth-century thinking. Freud considered himself a pioneering scientist, and yet a Gothic sensibility has been suggested at work across his work; Freud himself remarked how psychoanalysis behaves in an uncanny fashion.[16] In some ways the quintessential new science of the modern-age, psychoanalysis, obeys the logic of the Gothic plot, whereby the dark 'secrets' behind a patient's current psychoses lie buried in the past in the form of trauma, awaiting retrieval and resolution. Freud famously based his definition of 'the uncanny' on the German translation of the term 'unhomely', and the terror genre is often credited there as the first arena to have conceived of the haunted (*unheimlich*) house as a place possessing a kind of life of its own, a point emphasised by art historian Brian Dillon in the catalogue to *The Surreal House* (2010). As witnessed in the figure of Freud, unexpected points of contact exist between what are conventionally considered Modernist versus counter-Modernist positions, also observed when mapping the fluctuating, malleable evocations of Gothic: from Victorian to Modernist, from psychoanalytical to Surrealist.

1 Kenneth Clark, *The Gothic Revival: An Essay in the History of Taste* (1928) (London: John Murray, 1962), pp. 9, 8.

2 Andreas Huyssen, *After the Great Divide: Modernism, Mass Culture and Postmodernism* (1986) (Basingstoke: Macmillan, 1988), p. 56.

3 Clement Greenberg, 'The Present Prospects of American Painting and Sculpture' (1947), in *The Collected Essays and Criticism*, Vol. 2, ed. John O'Brian (Chicago: University of Chicago Press, 1996), p. 166.

4 Clement Greenberg, 'A Conversation in Three Parts with Trish Evans and Charles Harrison', in *Greenberg: Late Writings*, ed. Robert C. Morgan (Minneapolis and London: University of Minnesota Press, 2007), p. 197.

5 T. J. Clark, *Farewell to an Idea: Episodes from a History of Modernism* (New Haven and London: Yale University Press, 1999), pp. 316–17.

6 E. T. Marinetti, 'Futurist Speech to the English' (1910), in *Modernism: An Anthology*, ed. Lawrence Rainey (Malden, MA; Oxford; and Carlton, Victoria: Blackwell, 2005), pp. 8–9.

7 John Cage, 'Indeterminacy' (1958), in *Silence* (Middletown, CT: Wesleyan University Press, 1995), p. 261.

8 Andrea Fraser, 'Isn't this a wonderful place? (A Tour of the Tour of the Guggenheim Bilbao)', in *Museum Highlights: The Writings of Andrea Fraser* (Cambridge, MA and London: MIT Press, 2003), p. 233.

9 See A. G. W. Pugin, *Contrasts* (1836).

10 John Ruskin, 'The Nature of Gothic', in *The Stones of Venice* (1851–53), cited in *The Genius of John Ruskin*, ed. John D. Rosenberg (Charlottesville, VA and London: University of Virginia Press, 1998), p. 179.

11 André Breton, 'Limits Not Frontiers of Surrealism', in *Surrealism*, ed. Herbert Edward Read (London: Faber & Faber, 1936), pp. 110–11.

12 Theodor Adorno, 'Looking Back on Surrealism' (1956), in *Modernism: An Anthology*, ed. Rainey, p. 1114.

13 Georges Bataille, cited in *Surrealist Women: An International Anthology*, ed. Penelope Rosemont (Austin: University of Texas Press, 1998), pp. xli–xlii.

14 Clement Greenberg, 'Surrealist Painting' (1944), in *The Collected Essays and Criticism*, Vol. 1, ed. John O'Brian (Chicago: University of Chicago Press, 1986), p. 226.

15 Hal Foster, *Compulsive Beauty* (Cambridge, MA and London: MIT Press, 1993), p. 230n; pp. 280–81n.

16 'Indeed it would not surprise me to hear that psychoanalysis, which seeks to uncover these secret forces, had for this reason itself come to seem uncanny to many people.' Sigmund Freud, *The Uncanny* (1819), trans. David McLintock; intro. Hugh Haughton (London: Penguin, 2003), p. 150.

SHADES OF MODERN GOTHIC

N

—IS FOR—
NATIVES,
RESTLESS

Sonia Solicari is Head of Guildhall Art Gallery and London's Roman Amphitheatre, where she has curated numerous exhibitions, though is perhaps best known for her imaginative Gallery parties, on the occasional Friday night. Sonia has held the posts of Curator, Ceramics, and Assistant Curator, Paintings, at the Victoria & Albert Museum, and has written and lectured widely on the nineteenth century and Victorian revivalism. Sonia is the curator of *Victoriana: The Art of Revival*, at Guildhall Art Gallery (2013).

Catherine Flood lives on a boat in south west London from which she conducts her career as Curator at the Victoria and Albert Museum, specialising in posters, graphics and ephemeral print. Her dedication to all things Victorian has led her to publish widely on nineteenth-century print culture, including Victorian fashion plates and fashion satires and the social meanings of nineteenth-century catalogues and gallery guides. Catherine's work has also been known to stray into the twentieth and twenty-first centuries – she is the author of *British Posters: Advertising, Art and Activism* (2010).

Tom Gallant is an artist whose dramatic interpretation of Charlotte Perkins Gilman's 1892 novella, 'The Yellow Wallpaper', recently transformed the exhibition spaces of Danson House, London. Tom's work takes inspiration from Victorian decorative craft, particularly the revealing and concealing possibilities of paper cut and lace. He has studied Fine Art Print at Camberwell College of Art & Design and Graphic Design at Southampton Institute. Tom is currently working on a solo project: *Among These Dark Satanic Mills*, Manchester City Gallery (2015).

Lee Jackson is a little obsessed with the social history of Victorian London. He has written seven historical crime novels (published in the UK and France); two anthologies of Victorian daily life – *A Dictionary of Victorian London* (2005) and *Victorian London* (2004) – and, most recently, a guide to *Walking Dickens' London* (2012). He has an ever-increasing collection of photographs of the surviving parts of the Victorian metropolis and a shameless addiction to Twitter. He is currently working on a book for Yale University Press, provisionally titled *Dirty Old London*.

Cora Kaplan is Honorary Professor of English at Queen Mary, University of London and Professor Emerita of English at Southampton University. A feminist cultural critic and theorist, with a special interest in class and race, her work has focused on questions of aesthetics and politics in women's writing in Britain from the late eighteenth century through the mid-Victorian period. Her most recent book, *Victoriana: Histories, Fictions, Criticism* (2007) has been the inspiration for the exhibition *Victoriana: The Art of Revival* at Guildhall Art Gallery.

Tim Killick has written extensively about nineteenth-century literature and art – in particular the short story in the Romantic period and the Victorian illustrated book. He has previously worked as a researcher and lecturer at Cardiff University. His publications include *British Short Fiction in the Early Nineteenth Century: The Rise of the Tale* (2008), the online *Database of Mid-Victorian Wood-Engraved Illustration* (DMVI), and a scholarly edition of Allan Cunningham's *Traditional Tales of the English and Scottish Peasantry* (2012).

Matt Lodder is an academic art historian, based in London. His work is primarily concerned with the history of Western tattooing and the artistic status of body art and body modification practices. He teaches contemporary art and theory at the Universities of Reading and Birmingham and works as a freelance writer, speaker and broadcaster. His research interests include lowbrow, outsider, kitsch and erotic art and visual culture; internet and digital art; and the art, music, culture and philosophy of inter-war Paris. He is currently writing a book called *Tattoo: An Art History* for I. B. Tauris.

Katty Pearce was born about one hundred years too prematurely for her liking and in slightly the wrong place. Katty awaits the opportunity to begin again; until such time, she is Curator at Guildhall Art Gallery. Interests include many things you wouldn't expect, and some you would. Previous real life experience includes Keats House Museum, subtitling most of ITV including *The Jeremy Kyle Show*, various theatre dogsbodying, ill-advised dabblings in amateur journalism, and the odd (very) play.

Paul St George has long been fascinated by the abundance of inventions that bloomed at the end of the nineteenth century. Paul has discovered that a good few of these dormant inventions have a new relevance in the twenty first century. Paul's healthy obsession is to bring some of these latent glories to life and to draw out the connections between now and then. The Telectroscope is the biggest and best of these projects. Paul has just written his first novel, and is looking for a literary agent.

Matthew Sweet presents *Night Waves* and *Free Thinking* on BBC Radio 3 and *The Philosopher's Arms* and *The Film Programme* on BBC Radio 4. His books and TV programmes include *Inventing the Victorians, Shepperton Babylon, The Rules of Film Noir* and *Silent Britain*. His most recent, *The West End Front*, was a Radio 4 *Book of the Week* and is in development as a TV drama. His journalism appears in the *Guardian* and *Intelligent Life*. In the BBC2 film *An Adventure in Space and Time*, he plays a moth from the planet Vortis.

Otto Von Beach was born in 1857. His successful career as an artist was interrupted while on an expedition to Siberia in 1896. Swept away by a freak uphill avalanche, Otto lay frozen in the Russian ice for the next 114 years. Discovered by a passing hiker in March 2010, Otto's body was sent to Moscow for routine analysis. There, scientists were astonished to discover faint signs of life and immediate steps were taken to resuscitate him. He has since resumed his career as an illustrator and now shares a studio with his great-great-grandson and illustrator, Beach. Previous publications include *Who Moved my Stilton, Gin and Juice* and *W. G. Grace Ate my Pedalo*.

Sarah Waters is an award-winning novelist and doyenne of neo-Victorian literature. Her nineteenth-century inspired novels include *Tipping the Velvet* (1998), which won the Betty Trask Award; *Affinity* (1999), which won the Somerset Maugham Award and the *Sunday Times* Young Writer of the Year Award, and *Fingersmith* (2002), which won the *South Bank Show* Award for Literature and the CWA Historical Dagger. *Tipping the Velvet* and *Fingersmith* have both been adapted for BBC television and *Affinity* has been adapted for ITV. She has a PhD in English Literature and has been an associate lecturer with the Open University.

Gilda Williams was born in New York and has been based in London since 1994. Gilda currently works as a lecturer on the MFA in the curating programme at Goldsmith's College, University of London. Her anthology *Gothic* (MIT/Whitechapel) was published in 2007; her subsequent research on defining the contemporary Gothic aesthetic will be partially published in *The Gothic World* (eds Townsend and Byron, Routledge, 2013). Williams is a London correspondent for *Artforum* (since 2005) and a film reviewer for *Sight & Sound* (2000–09).

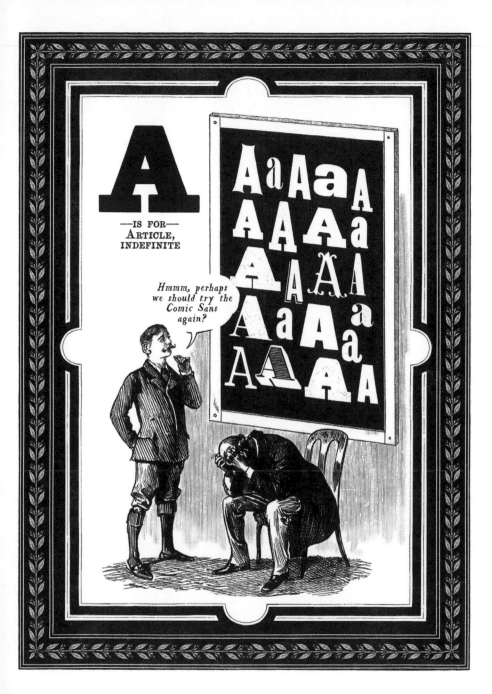